Blinded by the Whites

WHY RACE STILL MATTERS IN 21ST-CENTURY AMERICA

David H. Ikard

INDIANA UNIVERSITY PRESS   *Bloomington & Indianapolis*

This book is a publication of

INDIANA UNIVERSITY PRESS
Office of Scholarly Publishing
Herman B Wells Library 350
1320 East 10th Street
Bloomington, Indiana 47405 USA

iupress.indiana.edu

Telephone orders 800-842-6796
Fax orders 812-855-7931

© 2013 by David H. Ikard

∞ The paper used in this publication
meets the minimum requirements of
the American National Standard for
Information Sciences–Permanence of
Paper for Printed Library Materials,
ANSI Z39.48–1992.

*Manufactured in the
United States of America*

*Cataloging information is available from the
Library of Congress.*

ISBN 978-0-253-01096-4 (cloth)
ISBN 978-0-253-01103-9 (ebook)

1 2 3 4 5   18 17 16 15 14 13

To

TERRY TYRELL JOHNSON
(OCTOBER 28, 1996–AUGUST 27, 2012)

A life well lived

She did not tell them to clean up their lives or to go and
sin no more. She did not tell them they were the blessed of
the earth, its inheriting meek or its glorybound pure.

She told them that the only grace they could have was the grace they
could imagine. That if they could not see it, they would not have it.

Baby Suggs in *Beloved,* by Toni Morrison

Contents

Acknowledgments

ON AUGUST 27, 2012, MY FIFTEEN-YEAR-OLD NEPHEW TYRELL Johnson died in a car accident on the first day of school in his sophomore year. The driver of the car, sixteen-year-old Cody Rives, also died. A few weeks prior to his death, Ty visited Tallahassee, Florida, with his grandmother (my mother) to hang out with me and my two children, both of whom adored and idolized Ty. Little did I know this was going to be the last time I would see this extraordinary young man alive. A standout student and leader, Tyrell was mature beyond his years. He had come to visit, in fact, because he knew I was teaching summer school and wanted to sit in on my class to get a feel for what goes on in a college classroom. Though he was unfamiliar with most of the material I was teaching, he was visibly and intensely engaged for the entire hour and forty-five minutes of the class meeting. In addition to sitting through my class, we laced 'em up, went to the FSU gym, and played ball for an entire afternoon. As is always the case with the men in my family, there were lots of junk talking, laughing, and fade-away jump shots. We had a blast. Though a somewhat introverted teen, Ty was rather chatty that weekend, going on and on about obtaining his driving permit, an ROTC leadership camp he had recently attended, his older brother BJ, whom he deeply admired, his challenges with his divorced father and mother, both of whom struggle with substance abuse, and, more generally, about his future hopes and dreams. Later that weekend, we headed to the beach. The normally clear water at St. George Island – a public beach on the Gulf of Mexico – was laden with seaweed. Rather than deter us from playing in the water, the seaweed served as weapons of mischief – it was more fun than I can adequately articulate. Everybody played to the point of exhaustion. It was a good day indeed. When Ty and his grandmother left that Monday morning after gracing us with their presence for four days, I remember thinking to myself as the car pulled off how wonderful it was to have been able to spend such quality time with my nephew. He was becoming a man right before my eyes and it was beautiful to watch. I had no doubt that Ty would go on to do great things, that his future was bright. Then the call came about ten days later. It was my mother. Out of breath. Frazzled. Scaring me because I feared for her health. But when she gathered herself and told me the news, I heard myself screaming, "No, Mom! This cannot be real! Tell me this is not real!" "He's gone, David," she responded, as if not truly believing the words coming out of her mouth: "My baby is gone."

Though it's been several months now since his death, I think about Ty every day. I now see Ty's visit for what it was – a gift by the universe; my opportunity to make more memories with my nephew; to assure him that despite the familial obstacles he faced, he was going to be all right; that his uncle had his back. I even told him that he could stay with me the next summer – an offer, I later learned from my mother, that he was so excited about that one of the first things he did when he returned to North Carolina was to ask his father for permission to live with me the following summer. During his stay with me I told him about this book and promised to send him a copy when it was published. I also told him that he would be in the acknowledgments, as he had been in my previous books. He was floored. He didn't realize that his name was in print – that he'd been acknowledged. He was even more floored when I reached up on my bookshelf and showed him his name in the acknowledgment section of my first book. I was touched by his humility and pride.

When I spoke at Ty's funeral, I reminded his loved ones that his was a well-lived life; that more than mourning a life cut short, we should celebrate the fifteen wonderful years that we were able to be in his presence. When my son and first child, Elijah, was born, Ty was five years old. I was so enamored of my precocious nephew, whose favorite things were books and hugs; I remember telling my mother that if my son turned out nearly as well as Ty I'd be a very happy father. Indeed, Ty was the role model that I chose for my son or, perhaps more accurately, the role model my son chose on his own and which I wholeheartedly endorsed. "Don't you want to do well in school like Tyrell?" I would ask Elijah from time to time to keep him academically motivated. In recent years, however, it was Elijah who would invoke Tyrell as his intellectual muse, saying things like, "Dad, I can read almost as well as Tyrell!" and "Dad, do you think Tyrell would know the answer to this math problem? Grandma says he's a real math whiz." So, while my heart remains heavy, I choose to celebrate the short but beautiful life of my oldest nephew, Tyrell (Ty) Johnson. I dedicate this book to him as a way of memorializing his wonderful life. I miss you terribly, youngblood. You were a blessing. I'll see you on the other side.

There are many people to thank for making this book happen. My first shout out goes to my partner and brother from another mother, Martell Teasley. Besides being a brilliant scholar, dynamic teacher, eloquent speaker, visionary leader, and devoted father, Martell is the best friend a brotha could have. Though I've only known him for five years, I feel like I've known him my entire life. He's that brotha you can call in your darkest hour; that brotha who will tell you what you need to hear – even if it stings – rather than what you want to hear; that brotha who loves his people and wouldn't hesitate to die for his beliefs; that brotha who has forgotten more than you have read. You're an inspiration, Brotha Teasley. Thanks for always being there.

Much love also goes to that badass scholar par excellence Tracy Sharpley-Whiting, who exemplifies what it means to "profess." One of the most brilliant, accomplished, and relevant scholars putting it down today, Tracy has read and edited many drafts of this and other manuscripts of mine. Her comments and insights were invaluable to this project. I continue to marvel at her generosity of spirit and the care she takes to empower those around her. In a word, she is a BOSS. Thanks, Trace, for all that you do.

Shout outs also go out to my boy Mark Anthony Neal. He is *that* dude. Bold enough to call himself a ThugNiggaIntellectual, Mark has taught me how to stay on my grind, how to keep the haters at bay and remain focused on the work. Though he has every reason to have the big head, Mark remains one of the most humble and giving scholar-activists I know. What I most admire about Mark is his ingenuity. Year after year he finds a way to raise the bar – from creating the New Black Man blog, which has now become a clearinghouse for cutting-edge black scholar-activism, to his web media show, "Left of Black," which has created a much-needed venue for scholars and activists of color to discuss their work and its relevance to empowering the dispossessed. It was Mark who introduced me to Tracy Sharpley-Whiting, Bakari Kitswana, and Joan Morgan; Mark who wrote my job letters, my tenure binder letters, who put me on to the Scholars Network, encouraged me to venture out and begin my own blog, and has even thrown his immense support behind my graduate students. You're an inspiration, MAN.

I'd also like to show some love to my writing group, consisting of Alisha Gaines, an outstanding young scholar; Rhea Lathan, my adopted sister; and Richard Mizzell, a gifted historian. Though we've only been meeting for a short time, I have greatly benefited from the insights, experiences, and brilliance of this cohort. Thanks for putting it on the line every meeting and for remaining committed to producing scholarship that liberates and empowers.

Shout outs go to the Ford Foundation for always bringing the inspiration. This tremendous organization is filled with phenomenal scholars of color that help to keep me grounded and motivated. I also want to rep the Scholars Network. This great network of scholars of color committed to the health and wellbeing of black men and boys has not only opened my eyes to the tremendous challenges before us as it concerns empowering our communities, but it has renewed my resolve to speak truth to power in my scholarship. To our phenomenal leader, renowned social scientist Alford A. Young, I say godspeed. Your efforts are appreciated and your sacrifice of time is not in vain.

To my go-to sista scholars – Lisa Thompson, Wizdom Powell, and La Vinia Delois Jennings – I say thanks for your unrelenting support and love. To Lisa: thanks for making me laugh to keep from crying; for allowing me to bend your ear about my problems; for inspiring me as a parent; for reminding me that our flaws do not define us but rather serve to remind us to remain humble. To Wiz: thanks for always seeing the cup half full; for the generosity of compliments that put wind into my sails; for being such a positive spiritual force. To La V: thanks for showing me what it means to have grace under fire; for helping me to see that death is a new beginning rather than the end of things; for sharing the stories of your family with me; for saving me from myself when I was a starry-eyed upstart at the University of Tennessee–Knoxville.

I want to thank my family: I love you with all my heart. To my mother, Joan Ikard: thanks for raising me to be a warrior; for teaching me to stand up for myself and against the white power structures that would have de-railed my academic success had you not intervened and advocated on my behalf; for teaching me that I am beautiful, that being smart is cool, for that spectacular red velvet cake you made for me on my sixteenth birth-day that I got to eat all by myself; for loving me unconditionally. To this day when I am confronted by forces of injustice I say to myself, and often out loud, "I am Joan Ikard's child. I'm not someone you want to cross."

To my father: thanks for being a real father. Though we may never see eye to eye on some important issues, I know that you love me and have always rooted for my success. I remember the wicked fast car you helped me build for Cub Scouts – the one that brought home the blue ribbon in my troop. The pride that winning made me feel in that sea of whiteness. I remember the humiliation we endured at the state track competition on Wake Forest's campus in 1987. We were there to support my sister Regina. Our car broke down on campus. As we were repairing it a group of white college students in a red convertible taunted us with shouts of "watermelon" and "fried chicken." I had hate in my heart. You tried to teach me to forgive. I remember the countless lectures about money management that you delivered when I was growing up, lectures that stay with me still and that have been instrumental in my financial success. I pray that you will understand my reasons for airing dirty laun-dry herein; that you will see past the hurt and recognize that I speak out of love, not to shame or humiliate.

To my siblings Regina, Terry, Randy, Crystal, and Tiffany. Thanks for being in my life. To Terry, Ty's father, I say I am so sorry for your loss. Parents are not meant to bury their children. I hurt for you and pray that you will find a constructive way to cope. To Regina: Thanks for always sticking up for me; for being that giving aunt; for blazing the trail to col-lege and setting the standard of excellence. To Randy: Thanks for all your help over the years. I wish we could turn back the pages and begin anew. To Crystal: Don't forget you're beautiful, brilliant, and capable. Doubt is your worst enemy. To Tiffany: Remember that I believe in you; that your dreams are within reach. Thanks for opening up and being brave. You are a beast. I will never forget that vacation with your beautiful children JaKayla and Jamar at the beach in 2012. The fish. The turtles. The impromptu soul train line. It was a time.

I also want to thank, Bob Sloan, my tremendous editor at Indiana University Press. Not only do you have a kind soul, you are a dream to work with. Indiana is very lucky to have you! I would also like to thank the journals MELUS and *Palimpsest.*

Finally, I want to thank my beautiful children, Elijah and Octavia. If Ty's death did nothing else, it reminded me of how fortunate I am to be your father. Elijah: When I look in your eyes I see the future; I see possibilities; I see a younger version of myself looking back at me. Sometimes it breaks my heart, but most of the time I am inspired. Inspired to be a better father, a better man, and a better teacher. Know that I will always be your biggest fan. To Octavia, my beloved daughter: I marvel at your intelligence and beauty. Your nightly request for "a hug and a kiss" from Daddy is what keeps me going sometimes. I look in your eyes and see unconditional love. I see a daughter who loves her Daddy. I think of you as my miracle baby, because the doctors told your mother that we couldn't have any more children after Elijah; that the tubes were 98 percent blocked. There were many tears. And then you showed up; defiant, strong, and full of life. It was obviously meant to be. I'm so proud of you and your brother that I could burst.

BLINDED BY THE WHITES

Introduction: What Does Black Empowerment in the Twenty-First Century Look Like?

BY MOST CONVENTIONAL MEASURES OF EMOTIONAL STABILITY, Ralph Ellison's unnamed protagonist in *Invisible Man* is emotionally unstable or, to use street vernacular, downright crazy. Paranoid about racial conspiracies to the point of viewing the entire society – including other African Americans – as potential threats to his personhood and sanity, invisible man lives alone in a secret underground dwelling in Harlem. He spends the bulk of his time contemplating the racial crisis that has brought him to this low point in his life and that he sees as a threat to the social stability of the United States. Viewing his current status as temporary (he characterizes his social isolation as a "hibernation"), he plans to "return" to the surface and reenter society when he has unraveled the conundrum of his and society's racial predicament, with a strategy in tow that he has developed to help explode the status quo. To prepare for his social reentry and liberation strategy, he becomes a one-man corporate subversive, stealing electricity from the Monopolated Light & Power Company, a powerful, white-owned local utility company. To maximize the impact of his subversion and accommodate his perplexing and insatiable desire for light, he wires his ceiling with 1,369 energy-guzzling light bulbs. His ultimate goal is to wire the room so that he can install light bulbs on the walls and floors. There is also a violent component to invisible man's subversive behavior. A powder keg of pent-up racial rage, he brutalizes and nearly murders a white man he bumps into on the street at night for calling him an "insulting name."[1] Not the least bit remorseful, invisible man blames the white man for provoking the near-fatal assault, arguing that his violent response was

1

appropriate to the circumstances and that whites' willful blindness to, and social erasure of, African American humanity constitutes the true crime. Given such inexplicably reckless and self-defeating behavior, it is hard to imagine that even invisible man's family – who, as the reader recalls, had been scandalized by his grandfather's bombshell of a deathbed pronouncement, referring to himself as a racial "spy" and imploring his adult children to educate his grandchildren to use their social invisibility as a weapon against white oppression – would disagree with a characterization of his state of mind as "crazy." "So much wasted potential," I imagine them saying. "He could have made something of himself; been a teacher or, better yet, a doctor. Now, he's walking around at night picking fights with white folks, trying to get himself killed and stirring up trouble for the rest of us. He's crazy for sure – a walking time bomb that won't be long for this world."

I am, of course, being intentionally polemical here. We know as informed readers that invisible man is not "crazy." He only appears so because his experiences of racial crisis are illegible socially even to most blacks. In *Invisible Man* Ellison employs the discourse of craziness via his protagonist to throw light back on the pathological and self-destructive contours of white supremacist thinking and blacks' unconscious and conscious participation in it. Flipping the prescribed racial script, Ellison puts the "raced" aspects of social normalcy under the critical microscope. In short, he reveals that law-abiding and racially accommodating blacks – the kind invisible man resembled before his political awakening – suffer from a kind of social dis-ease caused by living under the thumb of an even more dis-eased group in whites who preach democracy, equality, and fairness on the one hand and sabotage those principles in their treatment of black citizens on the other. The political trajectory of the novel, then, resituates the tag of "craziness" or pathological behavior from the oppressed to the oppressors. To label invisible man as "crazy" is to affirm Ellison's political formulation.

At the narrative level, invisible man's chief challenge is to literally and metaphorically write himself and his racial predicament into being. As he announces at the outset of the novel, he seeks to prove that he is not a freak of nature or of history, nor a figment of (white) social imagination. It is against this political backdrop that Ellison implores us to (re)assess invisible man's motives and actions. We see invisible man as heroic, if only because he disavows the raced status quo pursuit of fame, fortune, and social respectability and charts an active (rather than reactive) mode of self-determination. Being "active" in this instance means that he turns the tables on Monopolated Light & Power (read: the white power structure), putting them on the run as they anxiously scramble to locate the source of the power loss. Whether invisible man's specific plans of subversion ultimately bear fruit is not nearly as significant politically as his willingness to challenge the status quo at the risk of misunderstanding, social alienation (across racial lines), and even death. This point becomes clear in the epilogue after invisible man has recounted his story to the reader and, in so doing, gained a clearer understanding of his racial predicament for himself, including the extent to which he (and blacks) are complicit in the status quo. He asserts, "Humanity is won by continuing to play in face of certain defeat."[2]

The political and mental breakthrough occurs for invisible man when the pursuit of freedom in the form of individual agency and communal empowerment eclipses material gain, social prestige, ideological accommodation, and physical safety. To signify on the popular civil rights song, "Oh, Freedom," being buried in his grave becomes preferable for invisible man to embracing a subordinate social status and living as a (mental) slave. Indeed, in the final analysis, he shifts from bitterness to measured hopefulness on the issue of black oppression because he discovers (via his reconstructive storytelling) that despite the enormous advantages that whites hold over blacks on the social, political, and economic fronts, whites depend heavily on black complicity in oppression to maintain power and the illusion of racial supremacy. When at the close of the novel the reader catches up with invisible man's thinking on this score, invisible man's chance encounter with the white millionaire and trustee of the college, Mr. Norton (who symbolizes parasitical white hegemonic male power), on the New York subway becomes more legible. We see invisible man's new insights on complicity, self-determination, white supremacy, and power embodied in Mr. Norton's feebleness and confused state of mind. Metaphorically speaking, Mr. Norton's exposed vulnerabilities reflect how intensely whites rely on black complicity in oppression. Moreover, invisible man's verbal confrontation – wherein he never as much as raises his voice in disagreement – reveals that despite blacks' subordinate social status and economic weakness, they can impose their will onto whites and force them into vulnerable postures. In a profound power reversal of their previous encounter, in which the politically naive and socially ambitious invisible man plays racial lackey to the self-assured and paternalistic Mr. Norton, invisible man holds the upper hand – at least ideologically – and dictates the terms upon which he engages the discourse of "race" and Mr. Norton. He tells the powerful and directionally challenged millionaire (who, tellingly, cannot recognize invisible man from their previous encounter) that the personal stakes of their parasitical racial relationship have radically changed. Not only is invisible man no longer mesmerized by whiteness or the promise of (provisional) black power therein, but he sees the tragedy that is Mr. Norton's delusion of superiority. Mr. Norton's fear of the delusion-free invisible man (he jumps on the first available train despite not knowing where it, or he, is going) suggests that invisible man has solved a key part of the equation of oppression. Whether his newfound social awareness and cultural knowledge will ultimately translate into substantive political change on the ground is an altogether different matter. If, as the protagonist tells Mr. Norton, all the "trains" to true (in)sight lead back to the Golden Day – the black insane asylum that houses several radical thinkers who, like invisible man, are misidentified as madmen – then the reader knows instinctively that the chances of transformative change on the ground are precarious at best.

While certainly unique in its engagement with the mental, emotional, and intellectual challenges of breaking through the ideological barrier and social policing of black inferiority/white supremacy for post-Reconstruction blacks, *Invisible Man* reflects a long political trajectory of such complex engagements within African American literature, dating back to slavery. Indeed, identifying and rooting out even more intense forms of this ideological barrier and social policing were dominant themes in slave narratives. We witness perhaps the most vivid and sophisticated account of this dynamic in Frederick Douglass's *The Narrative of the Life of Frederick Douglass*. To at once condemn slavery as morally evil and humanize the enslaved, Douglass turns the dominant idea of inherently primitive and pathological blacks and civilized, morally upstanding, and intellectually superior whites on its head. He offers a sophisticated sociological critique of policed white supremacy and the toll it takes on raced minds and bodies before the field of sociology as an academic discipline – and, specifically, the idea that we are products of our social conditioning – had even emerged. The transformative power of his critical insights becomes clear early on in the narrative when he explains why slaves tend to lie about their debilitating treatment and living conditions to whites and even themselves. To contextualize his claim, Douglass tells the story of a slave who mistakes his master as a passerby and lets his mental guard down, speaking the truth to the man about his abject social circumstances. As punishment for his truth telling and, more specifically, for his challenge to white supremacist myths about humane and just slaveholders, the slave is "sold to a Georgia trader."[3] Douglass expounds that the dangers of such truth telling extend beyond white spaces, as slaveholders plant "spies" among the slaves ranks to report "discontented" slaves. This added layer of policing intensifies an already high level of paranoia among the enslaved, leading many "to suppress the truth" about their suffering and white moral and ethical corruption as a means of survival. Douglass asserts that this brutal socialization so warps reality that enslaved blacks begin to conceptualize and evaluate their experiences of enslavement via the cultural lens of their oppressors. Elaborating on the effects of his own conditioning, Douglass writes, "I have been frequently asked, when a slave, if I had a kind master, and do not remember ever to have given a negative answer; nor did I, in pursuing this course, consider myself as uttering what was absolutely false; for I always measured the kindness of my master by the standard of kindness set up among slaveholders around us."[4] Douglass reveals that the institution of slavery not only encourages black complicity in oppression, but it directly manufactures it. Slaves' unconscious complicity in oppression represents for Douglass, then, a profoundly human response to an unconscionable assault on moral decency and human consciousness.[5] Flipping the racial script of inferiority/superiority, Douglass shows that the real savages and heathens are the pro-slavery whites that brutalize enslaved Africans into this self-defeating posture of complicity for material gain. What's more, Douglass registers that the path to what Paul Gilroy calls "self-creation" and "self-emancipation" pivots in large part on slaves' capacity to recognize and explode these designed patterns of unconscious complicity. Douglass embodies this political impulse when he reports his disgust at Master Hugh's gesture of giving him a tiny portion of his earnings back as an incentive: "I regarded it [Master Hugh's monetary incentive] as a sort of admission of my right to the whole. The fact that he gave me any part of my wages was proof, to my mind, that he believed me entitled to the whole of them. I always felt worse for having received any thing; for I feared that the giving me a few cents would ease his conscience, and make him feel himself to be a pretty honorable sort of robber."[6]

Though Douglass's escape strategy – which requires establishing a level of trust with Master Hugh – prompts him to hide his disgust, the reader clearly sees Douglass's epiphany. Having unraveled the link between white supremacist ideology and black complicity in oppression, Douglass is insulted rather than gratified by Master Hugh's dubious payoff. He knows that accepting the proffered gift means cosigning Hugh's distorted idea of himself as a good master. It is hardly surprising, then, that Douglass considers being "robbed" outright (that is, not receiving a monetary incentive) the lesser of two evils here.

Black women writers like escaped slave Harriet Jacobs usefully gender this discourse of breaking through the ideological and emotional barriers of institutional white supremacy. In *Incidents in the Life of a Slave Girl,* Jacobs reminds us that black women's gendered predicament of suffering during slavery was compounded by motherhood and, more vitally, the white pressure to procreate as a means to replenish the slave labor force and in turn increase the wealth of their enslavers. Exacerbating this predicament was the fact that white supremacist ideology constructed captive African women as seductive, hyperprimitive sexual beings. Indeed, a widely held belief at the time was that African women preferred sexual copulation with orangutans to humans. When sex occurred between white men and captive African women, the thinking went, African women and their primitive, corrupt sexual nature were to blame. White men emerged in this scenario as the true victims, which explains why the white master's wife in, say, Zora Neale Hurston's *Their Eyes Were Watching God* viciously attacks Nanny and holds her husband blameless for the racially mixed child resulting from Nanny's coerced sexual relationship with him. In a word, black women couldn't legally or conceptually be raped. Moreover, the laws were constructed so that white rape was not only sanctioned but rewarded. As we learn in *Incidents,* the social station of the mother determines that of the child, meaning that children born out of white sexual coercion and rape were slaves as well – a perverse manipulation of law, power, and patriarchy indeed. (Douglass also comments at length on this abusive practice in *The Narrative.*) Even though Jacobs manages to stave off her white would-be rapist, Dr. Flint, she does so at the expense of seeking out another prominent white man for protection and becomes pregnant. Hyperconscious of how such shrewd acts of self-determination may look to her target audience of middle-class white women (remember, white women's social value in the nineteenth century was tied to chastity and social respectability), Jacobs reminds the reader time and again that slavery prevented her from being chaste and socially respectable. If we judge Jacobs's actions by the political standards of her day rather than by the political expectations of the present moment, it becomes clear that her interrogations of white male power and appeals to humanity were revolutionary *despite* her investments in white patriarchal notions of white womanhood. She dared as a black captive and woman to speak about rape and sexual coercion when such accounts were not only hotly contested in the public domain by slave apologists, but also deemed uncouth for respectable women to even broach publicly, let alone engage critically at great length. Jacobs breaks through the ideological and emotional barriers of white supremacist ideology, then, by bearing witness to black women's rape at the hands of white men and demanding that her humanity as a black person and woman be recognized and respected by those in power.

While at the dawn of the twenty-first century white supremacist power has loosened its grip on black self-determination and personhood – due in no small measure to the types of political and social interventions that the aforementioned writers and their ilk orchestrated and inspired – it nevertheless continues to impose its will on black communities in insidious and life-altering ways. One would think that the election of the first black president would draw even more attention to such matters, but the reality is that in many ways Barack Obama's singular achievement has given political currency to the age-old (white) idea that we live in a postracial (read: postracist) society. As white race critic Tim Wise astutely points out, this idea of postracialism is hardly new. He writes that "in 1963, roughly two-thirds of whites told Gallup pollsters that blacks were treated equally in white communities. Even more along the lines of delusion, in 1962, nearly 90 percent of whites said black children were treated equally in terms of educational opportunity."[7] Here, Wise reveals the cognitive dissonance between popular white attitudes about racial progress and the actual racial progress that is happening on the ground. While we can – and should – see Obama's achievement as a sign that racial attitudes have shifted for the better in the twenty-first century, it is politically naive and dangerous to take this singular achievement as a sign that a seismic shift in racial attitudes has occurred in our society. Wise rightly cautions that "the triumph of individuals of color cannot, itself, serve as proof of widespread systemic change."[8]

The stubborn persistence of economic inequality between blacks and whites, racial profiling among the police, the attendant prison industrial complex, zero-tolerance laws and policies in schools (and beyond) that disproportionately target black and brown folks, racial health disparities, and the like demonstrate that what we are witnessing at this moment is not so much a radical shift in racial thinking but rather an updated version of white supremacist ideology. In effect, white supremacist ideology operates socially like a virus, constantly mutating and taking on new forms to remain alive and viable. So, just as a person never catches the same cold twice, but rather different mutations of the cold virus, black folks over the course of U.S. history have had to inoculate themselves against several versions of this ideology – versions that mutate and adapt in form, but not in substance, to the ever-shifting contours of our socioeconomic body politic. Invoking cultural theorist Stuart Hall on this score in his aptly titled book *How Race Survived U.S. History*, David R. Roediger writes that "racism emerges and is recreated from the imperatives of *new* sets of realities, not just from bad habits of the past; given this, the way that the Cadillac of white supremacy has undergone centuries of model changes, but no changes in substance,"[9] demands that we uncouple the lofty racial progress formulation from our past and present assessments of African American social advancements. A more strategically useful formulation for African Americans, in this instance, is one that adequately reflects the mutability of white supremacy over time and its continued centrality in shaping our national identity and public policies.

Blinded by the Whites: Why Race Still Matters in 21st-Century America addresses these new and more sophisticated forms of white supremacy to give voice to the challenges of self-determination, agency, and empowerment in general that continue to elude all but a select group of African Americans. Indeed, *Blinded by the Whites* was inspired in part by the conspicuous blind spots in media coverage on the state of black America during the Great Recession. Though black and brown folks were by far the hardest hit by subprime mortgage malfeasance, unemployment, and the loss of net value and the least to benefit from the TARP monies handed out to stimulate the economy, the mainstream media focused on the suffering of the white middle class. Politicians on the right and left, including President Obama, followed suit. In the meantime a large segment of black Americans suffered in silence, most so loyal to the president that they remained optimistic about their future and that of the country despite evidence to the contrary in their communities.[10] Consequently, the white supremacist ideology of postracialism/colorblindness that has long misinformed dominant white attitudes became even more entrenched because we had a black president. While the aforementioned assaults on black bodies and consciousness remain a problem in our society (in fact, wealth disparities between whites and blacks have returned to pre-1990s levels and continue to widen), the very language that we use to identify and resist these assaults is hijacked and politicized as racist.

Paul Beatty shines light on the absurdity of postracial/colorblindness thinking in *The White Boy Shuffle* in the scene in which the protagonist, Gunnar Kaufman – one of the few blacks attending his affluent elementary school in Santa Monica – sits through a lesson "on the importance of living in a colorblind society."[11] When Gunnar's paternalistic and shortsighted white liberal teacher Ms. Cegeny (Miscegeny) asks the class to offer examples of the "color-blind processes in the American society,"[12] the white students respond with answers like "justice" and "the [white] president of the United States," all of which the teacher applauds. When she calls on Gunnar to provide an example, he responds tersely, "Dogs." Oblivious to the racial critique in Gunnar's jocular response that colorblindness is a social fiction that covers over institutionalized white privilege and black suffering, Ms. Cegeny dismisses Gunnar's comments and implores her white class to judge (raced) groups by "their minds" rather than their "color." Beatty spells out his politics in the conversation that Gunnar has with the white school doctor about his recent lesson on colorblindness:

> "Our teacher says we're supposed to be colorblind. That's hard to do if you can see color, isn't it."
>
> "Yeah, I'd say so, but I think your teacher means don't make any assumptions based on color."
>
> "Cross on green and not in between."
>
> "They're talking about human color."
>
> "So?"
>
> "So pretend that you don't see color. Don't say things like 'Black people are lecherous, violent, natural-born criminals.'"
>
> "But I'm black."
>
> "Oh, I hadn't noticed."[13]

The Ellisonian joke here pivots on the fact that the white doctor is advising Gunnar about colorblindness as if he were white. The racial stereotypes that the white doctor tells Gunnar to "pretend" not to harbor makes little sense considering that as a black boy Gunnar is the primary target of such stereotypes. The absurdity on display in telling a black boy to pretend not to see himself and black folks as pathological, subhuman criminals illuminates the centrality of race to social consciousness.

The hidden-in-plain-sight reality here is that a postracial/colorblind society is unrealizable at this point in history because the discourse of white normalcy relies on the idea of black abnormality for its cultural capital. This discourse of white normalcy is not just raced, but classed, sexualized, and gendered as well. We see this reality borne out in society in the ways that welfare programs are associated in the public sphere with the black poor, and particularly unwed black mothers, when the reality is that whites comprise the majority of welfare recipients. In fact, this stigma has slowly shifted away from these stereotypes during the Great Recession – not necessarily because attitudes about unwed black mothers on government assistance have drastically changed, but because the number of whites reliant on such assistance has dramatically increased.

But, alas, the challenge of black self-determination, agency, and empowerment is also hindered by blacks' unconscious complicity in the white supremacist institutions of power – a phenomenon that makes mounting a campaign of resistance all the more challenging. Kobena Mercer elucidates this pattern of complicity, writing, "Dominant ideologies such as white-bias do not just dominate by universalizing the values of hegemonic social/ethnic groups so that they become everywhere accepted as the norm. Their hegemony and historical persistence is underwritten at a subjective level by the way ideologies construct positions from which individuals recognize such values as a constituent element of their personal identity and lived experience." Accordingly, "racism works by encouraging the devaluation of blackness by black subjects themselves."[14] Recalling Frederick Douglass's explanation of why slaves tend to lie to their masters and themselves about their debilitating circumstances as slaves, Mercer pinpoints the ways that blacks are conditioned to experience white supremacy as normalcy and police each other's behavior in accordance. The social and economic dominance of whites in society makes this discourse of normalcy all the more difficult to recognize. As Marxist theorist Terry Eagleton asserts,

> No dominant political order is likely to survive very long if it does not intensively colonize the space of subjectivity itself. No oppressive power which does not succeed in entwining itself with people's real needs and desires, engaging with vital motifs of their actual experiences, is likely very effective. Power succeeds by persuading us to desire and collude with it; and this process is not merely an enormous confidence trick, since we really do have needs and desires which such power, however partially and distortedly, is able to fulfill.[15]

Toni Morrison echoes this political sentiment of collusion insofar as institutionalized white supremacy is concerned in *Beloved*, when Paul D reflects on blacks' conditioned obsession with proving their humanity to whites:

White people believed that whatever the manners, under every dark skin was a jungle. Swift unnavigable waters, swinging screaming baboons, sleeping snakes, red gums ready for their sweet white blood. In a way, he thought, they were right. The more colored people spent their strength trying to convince them how gentle they were, how clever and loving, how human, the more they used themselves up to persuade whites of something Negroes believed could not be questioned, the deeper and more tangled the jungle grew inside. But it wasn't the jungle blacks brought with them to this place from the other (livable) place. It was the jungle whitefolks planted in them.[16]

Here, Morrison reflects a version of Du Bosian double consciousness through Paul D's insights on internalized white supremacy. When coupled with the material realities of racism, internalized white supremacy overwhelms blacks' critical consciousness, making it difficult to see their humanity beyond the imposed racial identity scripts. Because of these ideological and social variables, blacks tend to view themselves, or certain patterns of negative behavior that is socially tethered to blackness, as "the problem," to evoke Du Bois's language, rather than the pathological discourse of white supremacy that they have internalized. As a result of these conditioned blind spots, blacks are thrust into the social posture of having to prove and/or defend their humanity. Consider the tragic killing of unarmed teenager Trayvon Martin by a "white"[17] community watchmen, George Zimmerman. If the racial dynamics were reversed and Martin were white and his killer black, an arrest would have most certainly been made on the spot. Extant gendered and raced scripts about black men as inherently threatening and dangerous meant that Trayvon's parents and the mostly black communities that rallied around them were thrust into the position of having to "humanize" Trayvon in the eyes of the white public in order to get the state and federal governments to intervene. These conditioned blind spots also mean that blacks are pressed into evaluating their humanity through the eyes of their historic oppressors. As white supremacy – even the more sophisticated version(s) today – operates a priori on the notion that African Americans are inherently monolithic; the unflattering actions of the individual continue to have a major bearing on how whites perceive the collective. (This calculus only operates one way. That is to say that the high achievements of the individual – say Barack Obama or Oprah Winfrey – tend to be read as exceptions to the rule of black inferiority.) Blacks are thus encouraged to direct their venom toward those who are perceived as reinforcing black stigmas – thug rappers, pimps, sexual predators and the like – rather than the white-supremacist domains of power that invented, and invent, these stigmas and pit blacks against each other. Examples of this mindset abound today, from Bill Cosby's infamous claim that the black poor rather than white oppression is chiefly responsible for black underachievement in the twenty-first century[18] to Barack Obama's mind-boggling support of the Moynihan Report,[19] which characterized black culture as a "tangle of pathology" and blamed black women rather than systemic racial discrimination for emasculating black men.[20]

Blinded by the Whites aims to suss out and make legible this new and ever-shifting ideological discourse of white supremacy that frustrates black self-determination, agency, and empowerment in the twenty-first century. As mentioned earlier, we now live in a society where it is possible to elect a black man to the presidency of the United States and still remain socially mired in racial biases that allow a large segment of the black population to suffer in silence. Though I will employ a host of critical and interdisciplinary approaches to tackle these pressing issues, black feminism will loom large in my intellectual arsenal. Contrary to popular belief, black feminism concerns itself with empowering all oppressed groups, not just black women. Intersectionality – the foundational theory of black feminism – argues that all oppressions intersect and must be confronted in kind in order to upset status quo power. What black feminism exposes, then, are the intersecting variables of race, gender, class, and sexuality that inform and complicate our experiences of agency and self-determination in the public and private spheres. Black feminist women have used black feminist theory to clear a space in black communities and white feminist circles in order to be seen and heard as not just blacks, women, queers, mothers, and working-class individuals, but as a group that experienced multiple layers of oppression simultaneously. They rightly cautioned their "natural" allies in anti-racist black men, feminist white women, and even straight feminist black women that defending any form of privilege – whether it be patriarchy for black men, white privilege for white women, or heteronormativity for straight folks across race and gender lines – was detrimental to all efforts at combating oppression and discrimination.

And to be clear, black feminists have always rejected biological de-
terminism and been supportive of black men. Their beef is – and has
always been – with black men's investment in patriarchal thinking. Black
feminist scholar and critical race theorist Athena D. Mutua gives voice
to this political impulse in her groundbreaking anthology *Progressive
Black Masculinities*. She argues that black men are also disadvantaged by
gender – a phenomenon she calls "gendered racism."[21] The term denotes
the ways that black men are targeted, profiled, or discriminated against
by the police, school system, or potential employers because of their
intersecting subjectivities as blacks, men, and working class/poor.

Even as my first book, *Breaking the Silence: Toward a Black Male
Feminism Criticism,* took up many of the same political and ideological
concerns that I am broaching in this study, it did so with an eye toward
thinking primarily about black men's roles in black feminist criticism
and activism. *Blinded by the Whites* remains reliant on black feminist
critical perspectives as a guidepost but thinks more expansively about
what critical models need to be invented or redefined to better equip
black folks in general and scholar-activists in particular to navigate this
tricky new political and cultural terrain in which, for the first time in
history, select black folks can *genuinely* enjoy the spoils of elite white
access even as the majority of blacks face historic economic fallout. In
Blinded by the Whites I also think about how my subjectivity as a black
man, parent, brother, son of working-class parents, Southerner, first-
generation college student, and professor inform my critical perspectives and political choices. I am particularly reflective about my role as a
father to my ten-year-old son, Elijah, and six-year-old daughter, Octavia.
However idealistic it may be, I feel an incredible obligation to improve
the society in which my children live: to make it a place where they are
seen and heard as human beings, irrespective of their imposed racial,
gender, class, and sexual identities. The world in which my children will
be adults will certainly look different from the one in which I came of
age. People of color are projected to eclipse the white population in the
United States by as early as 2037. Judging from the recent explosion of
xenophobia and the legislative attacks against competing racial/culture
narratives of white dominance (Texas and Arizona come immediately

to mind), it is clear that theirs will be no less a challenge for being seen
and heard than was my own growing up in small-town North Carolina.

Engaging my subjectivity at the level of the personal also means
airing the dirty laundry of patriarchal and sexual abuses within my own
family that have altered my life and the lives of those nearest and dearest
to me in immeasurable ways. When one delves as deep into the personal
as I have in this study, there will inevitably be fallout. After all, weren't
we taught from childhood that airing dirty laundry was grounds for cultural and familial ostracism, that what goes on in this house stays in this
house? Yet, as Audre Lorde reminds us, speaking truth to power – however messy, incomplete, ugly, incoherent, or painful that truth may be – is
a necessary first step to emotional, intellectual, and cultural growth: "I
have come to believe over and over again that what is most important to
me must be spoken, made verbal and shared, even at the risk of having it
bruised or misunderstood."[22]

Stuart Hall also reminds scholar-activists that intellectual and political growth goes hand in hand with self-analysis and critique. If a scholar-
activist does not feel the tension between the intellectual work that they
do and the material and social outcomes – or lack thereof – that it has
on the ground, then "theory has let you off the hook."[23] Hall expounds
on the paradox: "I want to suggest a different metaphor for theoretical
work: the metaphor of struggle, of wrestling with angels. The only theory worth having is that which you have to fight off, not that which you
speak with profound fluency."[24] In many regards, Hall's idea of "fighting
off" theory, of wrestling with (mis)understanding and viewing intel-
lectual/political discomfort as a healthy state of mind, encapsulates my
political impulse in *Blinded by the Whites*. What becomes clear is that
intellectualizing about the politics of breaking cultural silences is a far
cry from actually doing so. The personal stakes couldn't be higher.

Blinded by the Whites is divided into six chapters, each of which focuses on the new iterations of white supremacist ideology in the twenty-
first century, including postracialism and colorblind politics, and how
they inform and complicate lived experience and self-determination in
black spaces. In chapter 1, my aim is to push against a widely held perspective regarding Edward P. Jones's novel *The Known World*. The story

centers around the little-known fact that a few blacks owned slaves, a narrative that is dangerous and misleading because, in highlighting black complicity in slavery, it lets whites – past and present – off the hook for oppressing blacks. I argue that Jones, who is very conscious of and resistant to trivializing black suffering, has a very different political agenda. Namely, he seeks as a means of black empowerment to complicate in useful ways how black and white subjectivities are represented in history. Delineating his characters in a way that allows readers to see their intersecting subjectivities as raced, gendered, and classed beings, Jones demonstrates why such a dehumanizing and pathological discourse as white supremacy is emotionally and ethically toxic even for the whites who invent and police it. Hardly trivializing black suffering, Jones's representation of elite black slaveholders provides a model for thinking about the high stakes of class privilege and power within black spaces and the attendant dangers of seeing white supremacy – past and present – as normative.

In chapter 2, my purpose is to think about the practical application of black feminist principles in the twenty-first century. Using Toni Morrison's treatment of black men, white supremacy, and patriarchy in *Beloved* as a touchstone, I investigate the challenges of getting black men to think critically about gender subjectivity beyond the ways in which it disadvantages them. Because gender identity is constructed and policed at the intersection of the personal and political, I share my own experiences and challenges of coming to feminism as a black man and the son of what Mark Anthony Neal calls a "Strong Black Man." What I convey are the ways in which black feminist theory helped me to contextualize and move past the blind spots of the patriarchal abuses – including my father's socially sanctioned molestation of my aunt – that I witnessed growing up in my ultra-religious Southern household. Concomitantly, I also engage the gendered shaming discourses that keep black men from considering alternative anti-sexist masculine postures.

Focused on Paul Beatty's satirical treatment of black boys, sexual molestation, incest, white supremacy, and manhood in *The White Boy Shuffle,* in chapter 3 I undertake to expose the invisible realities of black men's emotional vulnerability and the social and cultural obstacles that complicate prescribed gender roles for black men. Of particular interest is Gunnar's brutal rape at the hands of his father, a self-hating LAPD police officer who displaces his feelings of white emasculation and white oppression onto his son. I argue that the stilted and obscure ways in which Beatty introduces Gunnar's incest rape in the novel highlight the challenges facing black men, including the author, when they broach and engage this gendered taboo issue.

In chapter 4 I come at the issue of white supremacy and black self-determination from the gendered standpoint of educating black boys to reject patriarchal and heteronormative modes of black male identity. Recalling my own challenges as a parent trying to educate my young son Elijah in this way, I address the ever-shifting social and cultural landscapes that frustrate redeeming masculine identities for young black men. I pay particular attention to the Trayvon Martin tragedy, not only because it maps out the ways our society continues to police and assault black male bodies, but because it presents a unique opportunity to re-think black men's gendered subjectivity as sexual and sexualized beings. Building on Kobena Mercer's arguments about the complex dialectics of power and subordination that inform black men's negotiations of white male hegemonic power, I argue that black men who traffic in heteronor-mative and hypermasculine notions of black men – like CNN pundit Roland Martin, who has been on the frontlines of the fight to bring justice to Trayvon Martin's family – give currency to the very notions of thug masculinity that they repudiate. I conclude then that empowering the next generation of black men will require more than just fighting against the white supremacist status quo; it will take exploding the notions of manhood that are reinforced and policed by many black men.

In chapter 5 I refocus the gender debate of empowerment onto black girls, and specifically onto the ideological challenges that they continue to face within and beyond white spaces in terms of making their complex humanity, intellect, and beauty legible beyond white gendered scripts of normativity. This perspective provides an opportunity to think criti-cally about how blacks generally, and black men in particular, can play a positive role in empowering black girls. I argue that while the urgency in black spaces to focus on black men's issues is understandable, given the dire socioeconomic circumstances of black men and boys in this country, such urgency often comes at the expense of ignoring the plight of black women and specifically black girls.

In chapter 6 I investigate how white surveillance continues to alter the ways that blacks react to unflattering racial portraits, even those that emerge from within critical black spaces. Though many (elite) African Americans see the film *Precious* – which is based on Sapphire's novel PUSH – as airing dirty laundry and reinforcing pathological notions of black consciousness, their perspectives reveal more about appeals to black respectability and the tenacity of extant white supremacist discourses than about the political motives of the movie. To wit, I argue that the movie demonstrates that systemic white oppression is debilitating in every way, often bringing out the worst, socially, culturally, and spiritually, in the oppressed. Moreover, as white-supremacist discourse obscures the past and present abuses of white power that have pressed blacks generally and black women in particular into subordinate social and economic status, blacks appear inherently pathological and deserving of white surveillance, paternalism, loathing, fear, policing, and violence. I conclude that, however flawed, *Precious* presses us to wrestle with the emotional, social, and economic outcomes of extant white power, including its debilitating effects on black consciousness and behavior.

Ultimately, *Blinded by the Whites* recognizes that black empowerment in the twenty-first century is an increasingly complicated affair. Encouraged as we are to see our society as not just postracial but *post-oppressive*, it becomes difficult – especially for African American youth and young adults – to reconcile their lived experiences and the micro- and macroagressions they endure on a daily basis with the master narratives of inclusiveness and egalitarianism that often trivialize or discount those experiences. *Blinded by the Whites* introduces critical frameworks that will hopefully shine light on these real challenges and provide useful ways of navigating our new and complex cultural landscape. What the recent tragedy of Trayvon Martin reveals is that such scholar-activism is still sorely needed. The fight to bring attention to his senseless death was waged, in part, on an intellectual front. Proponents of Martin had to find the language and critical models to flip the postracialist script that turned an innocent black teen into a violent criminal and the armed "white" neighborhood watch captain who stalked and killed him into a victim. The insightful commentary that grew out of this tragedy – the sharpest of which echoed black feminist principles of inclusion and intersectionality – was certainly up to the task. George Zimmerman was finally arrested (though not convicted), and the racially biased, NRA-inspired stand your ground law (which the Sanford police and district attorney used to justify setting him free in the first place) is under intense state and federal scrutiny. What this tragedy also demonstrated was that African American youth and young adults are as politically awake and engaged as ever. Indeed, they played a key role on the social media front in keeping this story alive. Even as it remains to be seen whether these protests on behalf of the Martin family will develop into a larger movement to, say, end racial profiling, the prison industrial complex, and skewed self-defense laws, one thing is for certain: grassroots activism can still be politically transformative. This is as true now as it ever was. I'm banking this book on it.

Henry had always said that he wanted to be a better master
than any white man he had ever known. He did not understand
that the kind of world he wanted to create was doomed before
he had even spoken the first syllable of the word *master*.

The Known World, Edward P. Jones

"I did not own my family, and you must not tell people that I did. I did
not. We did not. We owned . . . " She sighed, and her words seemed to
come up through a throat much drier than only seconds before. "We
owned slaves. It was what was done, and so that is what we did."

The Known World, Edward P. Jones

ONE

White Supremacy Under Fire: The Unrewarded Perspective in Edward P. Jones's *The Known World*

THE SEXUALLY CHARGED RELATIONSHIP THAT CLARA MARTIN, a white widow, has with her lone slave Ralph in Edward P. Jones's *The Known World* will strike most readers as schizophrenic. Though she is intensely attracted to Ralph, she goes to mental and social extremes to resist acknowledging her feelings even as she continues to actively pursue him. The event that throws her into this chaotic state of resistance occurs on the first night of a three-day-long storm when, after struggling to comb her wet, thick, unruly hair, she consents to Ralph's compliment-laced offer to do it for her. Finding the experience both emotionally comforting and intensely erotic, Clara allows him to groom her hair again over the next two nights. When the storm ends she discontinues the grooming without explanation. Shortly thereafter, she conjures up the notion that Ralph is secretly plotting to rape and murder her. At one point, after reading a local newspaper account of a slave, out of spite, putting finely ground glass in her master's food, Clara becomes so suspicious of Ralph, who has been her cook for twenty-four years, that she abruptly stops eating the food he prepares and loses weight as a result. In addition to declining to eat his food, she has Ralph interrogated, albeit with pointed directives not to "hurt his feelings" or "say anything mean," by first the slave patrollers and then John Skiffington, the sheriff of Manchester County, neither of whom find evidence of "wrongdoing."[1] Eclipsing the unfounded need to investigate Ralph's behavior, she begins a nightly ritual of nailing shut her bedroom door and sleeping with two knives – one by her bedside and the other under her pillow "as close as a lover."[2] Despite her expressed fears about Ralph's motives, Clara col-

21

lapses into an emotional state of panic after slavery is abolished and Ralph announces that he plans to leave Virginia and go live with his extended family in Washington, D.C. The narrator reports that Clara "cried and cried" when Ralph informed her of his plans to move, entreating him like a desperate lover to remain with her in Virginia.[3]

Clara's white crisis is hardly unique in *The Known World*; it is emblematic of a salient pattern of white identity crises in the novel, afflicting white-identified groups from across class, caste, and gender lines. Neither Barnum Kinsey, the poorest white man in Manchester County, nor William Robbins, the richest, escapes this fate. White supremacist ideology – the root cause of these white identity crises – penetrates the ethical and cultural fabric of antebellum society like secondhand smoke, contaminating the best of intentions by whites to treat African Americans humanely and even igniting white-on-white dehumanization and lethal action. Though the high stakes of legalized freedom complicate the ways that African Americans – slave and free – negotiate their agency as "othered" subjects within white supremacist ideology, those who seek status and economic gain within its strictures suffer similar crises and fates as their white counterparts.

Even as it is illuminating and rich, the scholarship on *The Known World*, in its paucity, does not directly engage white male supremacist ideology or the various identity crises across race, gender, and class lines that it engenders. Most scholars focus on ways in which the novel corrects, challenges, and/or rewrites the master narratives of slavery and African American struggle at large. Katherine Clay Bassard and Susan V. Donaldson's foundational analyses on *The Known World* reflect this trend in focus. Bassard maps the history of black slave-ownership with an eye toward debunking various raced and gendered myths about African American slave-owners. She uses her framework to explain why even benevolent participation in the system, such as buying relatives and loved ones out of slavery, reinforced rather than challenged status quo power relations. More specifically, she argues that former slave Augustus Townsend's act of buying his wife Mildred and son Henry out of slavery is neither redemptive nor threatening to the white male power structure. This reality is borne out in what she calls Augustus's tragic (mis)education of Henry, who becomes a prominent slave-owner.

Donaldson focuses primarily on Jones's interrogation of the idea of mastery at different social registers. Situating the novel as a postmodern neo-slave narrative, she argues that it seeks to problematize and revise master narratives of history while remaining keenly aware of its own provisional authoritative status. Donaldson concludes that the novel's postmodern disruption of history and authority provides the reader with "brief glimpses of the diminished sense of self and world allocated to enslaved people."[4]

Filling a gap in the scholarship as it pertains to white supremacist ideology and social consciousness, this chapter will examine the ways that white supremacist ideology goes "awry" and wreaks havoc in the lives of the white-identified groups it was ostensibly designed to empower, as well as to the Africans who adhere consciously and unconsciously to its twisted racial calculus. More specifically, it scrutinizes the power and class disparities within and across race lines that shape the experience of "race," revealing the wide-ranging stakes involved for adherents to white supremacist ideology with varying levels of agency, self-awareness, moral anxiety, and incentives to oppress and/or identify with oppressors. It becomes clear on one level that white male supremacy covers over rather than collapses the disparities of power among disparate European groups in the United States – namely, by unifying disparate classes of European settlers through denying rights and legal protection to Africans.[5] While the white supremacist racial discourse was, to quote Richard Dyer, "terrifyingly effective in unifying coalitions of disparate groups of people,"[6] Jones makes clear that it also warped Eurocentric critical perspectives on Africans, Native Americans, and ultimately other Europeans.

By making these socioeconomic dynamics of whiteness visible and treating white supremacy as a pathological mindset run amok, Jones's *The Known World* builds on and extends a longstanding liberating strategy in the African American literary tradition[7] that "trac[es] the corrupting effects of absolute sovereignty on owners of human chattel and on the individual psyches of slaves exposed to the abuses of that power."[8] Jones makes a unique contribution to this liberating strategy by using the history of African American slave-owners to bring renewed scrutiny to the tenacity and corruptive force of white supremacist ideology on

our nation's collective racial consciousness. Resembling what trauma
theorist Ron Eyerman calls a cultural "intellectual,"[9] Jones casts light on
and attacks normative white supremacy in the contemporary moment
by resituating it within established historical narratives as a pandemic of
the perverse. Through this narrative prism, Jones demonstrates that the
small pocket of African Americans that willingly participate in slavery
in *The Known World* are a reflection, in large part, of the tenacity and
corrupting apparatus of white (male) supremacist ideology on African
American consciousness. In such an ideologically warped milieu, where
African Americans are socially conditioned to see white dominance and
the brutal exploitation of black bodies for capital gain as natural, the
emergence of African American slaveholders becomes a radical indictment against white (male) supremacist ideology.

As *The Known World* has come under fire in the public domain for
perpetuating the very dynamics of white male supremacy under scrutiny
in this chapter, a survey of Jones's political motives is in order. As he
asserts in his essay "We Tell Stories," Jones's chief political aim for writing the novel was not specifically to draw attention to the little-known
historical fact about African American slave-owners. Rather, he wanted
to explore the social variables that prompt African Americans – then and
now – to turn "against their own kind" for individual gain.[10] He explains
that the "kernel" for writing the novel actually was his dismay, while a
college student in the 1980s, at the "political climate at that time" that
encouraged this self-sabotaging behavior.[11] To put the matter plainly,
the historical reality of slave-owning African Americans – which he discovered while studying the Holocaust and Jewish turncoats as a teenager – came into play as a focal point of the novel several decades *after* he
first gained knowledge of the practice. Moreover, he viewed the willingness by some to sell out their African Americans peers as deviant – not
representative – of African American behavior in the face of white oppression. He ostensibly set out as a writer to examine the socialization
process (i.e., internalized white supremacy) that corrupted their moral
and cultural outlooks. Writing about the historical reality of African
American slave-owners was for Jones a useful starting point for engaging
such patterns of complicity and internalized white supremacy in the present day. He notes forthrightly, "Had there been no black slave-owners

ever in America, I would not have felt the okay to venture out and manufacture a time and place where they did."[12]

The conspicuous critical silence on *The Known World* – most notably among African American scholars – is no doubt attributable the ways in which such engagements with African American complicity in oppression so easily become political fodder for the extant discourse of white denial. Within this discourse, which displaces the blame for slavery and African American suffering onto African American communities, African American acknowledgement of intraracial failings (such as those that lace the conciliatory rhetoric of, say, President Barack Obama) emerges as "evidence" of African American culpability and white innocence. Further complicating matters is a longstanding white capitalistic practice in the United States of rewarding African Americans – financially and otherwise – for reinforcing white stereotypes of African American pathological behavior.[13] Indeed, though the existence of African American slave-owners is news to most Americans, slavery apologists have long tried to use such information to represent slavery as a benign and civilizing experience for Africans and/or to suggest that Africans pathologically sold their own kind into slavery during the transatlantic slave trade. The latter argument, of course, ignores the salient reality that Africa – like Europe and Asia – is, and has always been, an extremely diverse cultural space. It also conspicuously ignores that Europeans invented the idea of a monolithic African culture to serve their imperialist objectives.[14] African Americans within and beyond academe have overwhelmingly shouldered the burden of dispelling these and other white distortions of U.S. history and slavery, especially as they concern pathologizing African American consciousness. Though Jones is fiercely committed to fighting against this tide of racial distortion as well, his status as an African American writing about African American slave-owners and complicity in oppression renders his novel vulnerable to white apologists' claims of white innocence and black culpability. The problem arises, however, when readers confuse this unavoidable racial trap with Jones's motives for writing the novel, a dynamic he confronts frequently in the public domain.[15]

Issues of intentionality and critical receptivity aside, James Baldwin's critique of white (male) supremacist ideology in *The Fire Next Time* provides a useful framework for unpacking the political impulse in *The Known World*. In *Fire* Baldwin treats white supremacy as a social cancer that gnaws away at the ethical fabric of white-identified America, making it difficult for whites to reconcile their inhuman and exploitative behavior toward African Americans and, by extension, toward each other. He notes that African Americans are largely protected from this cancer, at least so far as it causes them to lose their grip on material realities, because they are not mired down mentally with constructed white mythologies, including "that their ancestors were all freedom-loving heroes, that they were born in the greatest country the world has ever seen, . . . that Americans are invincible in battle and wise in peace, that Americans have always dealt honorably with Mexicans and Indians and all other neighbors or inferiors, that American men are the world's most direct and virile, [and] that American women are pure."[16]

Baldwin explains that these "white mythologies" produce a kind of ideological schizophrenia that keeps whites in emotional conflict with themselves regarding their self-worth. Invoking the metaphor of a mirror to denote the reality of white frailty that white-identified groups seek desperately to avoid by displacing their "unspeakable, private fears and longings" onto African Americans, Baldwin writes:

> All of us know, whether or not we are able to admit it, that mirrors can only lie, that death by drowning is all that awaits one there. It is for this reason that [African American] love is so desperately sought [by whites] and so cunningly avoided. Love takes off the masks that we fear we cannot live without and know we cannot live within. I use the word "love" here not merely in a personal sense but as a state of being, or a state of grace – not in the infantile American sense of being made happy but in the tough and universal sense of quest and daring and growth.[17]

Though Baldwin is somewhat totalizing in his perspectives on whites' identity crises and African Americans' insulation from them, he usefully identifies a pattern of racial interdependence that is crucial to understanding how white supremacy operates beyond the social and economic power to oppress. He shows that for white-identified people to maintain the illusion of biological racial supremacy, they must work consciously and unconsciously not to see African American personhood, nor to see the lie that they possess a superior mindset. This "not-seeing" is compounded by their desire to be "loved" unconditionally by the targets of their oppression and to be released from the burden of living up to an impossible standard of superiority.

In *Playing in the Dark: Whiteness and the Literary Imagination*, Toni Morrison echoes Baldwin's ideas when she discusses Mark Twain's *Huckleberry Finn* and what she calls the "parasitical nature of white freedom."[18] Highlighting Twain's problematic characterization of Jim, a runaway black slave, Morrison argues that even underclass whites, like Huck, who are marginalized or "othered" from mainstream bourgeois white society, depend parasitically on imagined African American inferiority to affirm their racial identity and humanity. In this particular instance, Twain creates in Jim a runaway slave with a "limitless store of love and compassion" for Huck and white masters, who believes that "whites are what they say they are, superior and adult."[19] Morrison asserts that Twain's "representation of Jim as the visible other can be read as the yearning of whites for forgiveness and love."[20] The problem is that this "yearning is made possible *only* when it is understood that Jim has recognized his inferiority (not as slave, but as black) and despises it."[21] Morrison writes that Jim's slave status and pathological self-hate not only make "play and deferment [of our judgment against Huck for treating him cruelly] possible – but they also dramatize, in style and mode of narration, the connection between slavery and the achievement (in actual and imaginary terms) of freedom."[22] Huck's liberation from the stuffy and pretentious classed codes of middle-class whiteness requires in Twain's formulation that Jim remain enslaved and in awe of whiteness. The pressing question that emerges for Morrison is not what Jim's contradictory impulses and actions tell us about African American identity. Rather, why do Mark Twain, Huck, and Tom so desperately need Jim's blackness to be inferior in order for them, as whites, to feel human and free?

Jones brings this parasitical racial equation to the forefront, portraying whites and, to a lesser extent, middle-class African American slave-owners as "slightly mad victims of their own brainwashing."[23] The reader is thus able to witness the extent to which the slave-owners displace their moral panic, sexual perversities, emotional insecurities, and savage behaviors onto the enslaved. Read against this ideological backdrop, it becomes clear that Clara Martin's invented image of her slave Ralph as a rapist and murderer-in-waiting reflects her own racialized anxieties, if not outright racist fears, about her intense emotional and physical attraction to him. To invoke Toni Morrison's apt phrasing, the "subject" of Clara's "dream [or nightmare in this instance] is [always] the dreamer."[24] The culprit here, at least insofar as it involves Clara's twisted racial mindset, is internalized white supremacy. To be precise, Clara cannot productively negotiate her emotional and sexual intensity toward an African American man because it directly and dangerously clashes with her internalized notions of white, male-sanctioned womanhood. In effect, Clara is at war within herself on both a conscious and an unconscious level. She wants, in a sexual relationship with Ralph, a level of intimacy that she cannot have without jeopardizing her physical safety or her illusory security of gendered virtue. We witness in her schizophrenic behavior toward Ralph an emotional manifestation of her ideological investment in white supremacy. To acknowledge her affection toward Ralph is for Clara to give into her baser desires and relinquish the cultural variable that registers her social worth in the white male hierarchy. To deny her affection is to subject herself daily to the burden of extreme self-policing and to contend with the anxiety that, despite her best efforts, she may be found out.

Patricia Yeager offers additional insights into why Southern slaveholders like Clara cannot acknowledge the personhood of their victims. Appropriating psychologist Christopher Bollas's formulation of the "unthought known" (the psychological process by which children negotiate events in their lives for which they have no viable conceptual basis), Yeager argues that the "nature of everyday southern thought" is bound up psychologically in "arrested systems of knowledge," allowing whites to avoid having to come to terms with African American suffering and humanity by refusing to attach a meaning to the act of oppression. To be anchored ideologically in white Southern culture, then, is to refuse to "think about what one already knows" about racial atrocities and to know, without being directly instructed, "what can be consumed . . . as knowledge and what cannot."[25]

We see this phenomenon of the unthought known at work in *The Known World* when Clara awakens from Ralph's sleep-inducing scalp massage and calls out to him three times before becoming "aware of a silence that seemed to have a kind of voice" telling her that "there was something wrong in calling him like that."[26] Clara reacts to this "voice" by abruptly "clos[ing] her mouth," even though she indulges in the intimate grooming ritual for two more days afterward. Jones's characterization of Clara's mindset as she reacts to her own transgressive thoughts is instructive here, highlighting her "refusal to think about what [she] already knows" about her sexual and emotional attraction to Ralph, an attraction that she refuses to name or to assign meaning. The reader sees this refusal when Clara glaringly misrepresents the sexual and emotional tension that exists between herself and Ralph to John and his wife Winifred as "miasma" or "bad air" between them. That she feels compelled to give voice to her feelings at all is indicative of the intensity of her emotional and physical arousal. Indeed, her feelings are so all-consuming and incommensurable with her gendered white supremacist identity that she needs to acknowledge them via misnaming to fortify her socially scripted *un*reality and reaffirm her social value as a "virtuous" woman within the white, male-centric community. She seeks out John, the metaphorical embodiment of white hegemonic manhood, for protection, but when pointedly asked by John over dinner to pinpoint the cause of her suspicions, conspicuously omits her most intimate physical contact with Ralph during the three-day rainstorm. We can read this omission as a semi-conscious application of the unthought known. Even though Clara does not assign meaning to her feelings for Ralph, she is aware enough about racial and genders codes not to introduce an issue that has the potential to be "misinterpreted" and invite serious scrutiny of her relationship with Ralph. In the end, her unthought known negotiations yield the desired outcome. She is able to remain in good standing with the embodiment of white male power in Skiffington without necessarily having to jeopardize the unthought known pleasures of her erotic interactions with Ralph.

Jones shows that securing her relationship to power imprisons more than frees Clara emotionally and socially. Even though accommodating the status quo insulates Clara from potential social scandal and eases her racial consciousness, it also renders her complicit in her own gendered subjugation and keeps her locked out from true emotional agency – namely, the freedom to acknowledge her feelings for Ralph privately and publicly. As a legal matter, married white women in the antebellum South were the properties of their husbands through the law of coverture. So, despite being white, their access to power over African American bodies was directly tied to accommodating white men. Rather than foster empathy with the racially oppressed, this phenomenon of gendered commodification heightened in many ways white women's socioeconomic allegiance to white male hegemonic power. As Hazel Carby explains, white women during the antebellum era viewed their power relationship with slaves through the social prism of race rather than gender, meaning that they accepted the unspoken white male bargain of subordination in exchange for provisional power over the enslaved. Carby concludes that this "dependence on the [white] patriarchal system" prompted white women to identify their "interests with the maintenance of the status quo."[27] For Clara, this means literally and figuratively nailing herself into the ideological prison of complicity in oppression and cutting herself off from a potentially life-enriching sexual and emotional relationship with Ralph. Her investment in this patriarchal system also means that she must, by necessity, assassinate Ralph's character and make him over as a monster to secure her claims to provisional power. This parasitical negotiation of white supremacy and womanhood transforms Clara into a version of the psychopath that she imagines Ralph to be.

Considering that Ralph stays on with Clara after slavery is abolished, it is clear that he too has an ideological and emotional stake in this parasitical relationship. Though Jones does not provide us with a full account of Ralph's perspective, his omniscient narrator encourages readers to see Ralph's gestures of affection and loyalty as transcendent rather than tragic. We learn, for instance, that Ralph's original intent after slavery is to reunite with family in Washington. Crucially, he alters these plans and decides to stay put *after* Clara drops her gendered racial guard and tearfully begs him to stay with her. Moreover, once Clara dies, Ralph is able to move on without bitterness and find tranquility among his relatives.

If Clara's raced anxiety over her true feelings for Ralph dramatizes the extent to which internalized white male supremacy complicates the experience of womanhood for white women, slave patroller Barnum Kinsey's raced anxiety over his forced participation in selling Augustus – a free African American man – back into slavery dramatizes the extent to which internalized white male supremacy complicates the experience of white manhood for working-class white men. Jones registers the gender and class complexity of Barnum's white manhood by reminding us repeatedly that Barnum, the town drunk, is the poorest man in Manchester County and that in the eyes of his white peers he is considered "little more than a nigger."[28] Jones's message to the reader is that Barnum is "white trash" and is thus not fully entitled to the socioeconomic spoils of white hegemonic manhood. As Annalee Newitz and Matthew Wrays observe, to be marked as white trash is to be raced and classed as the white other and socially excluded from "the core of [acceptable] whiteness" and full access to white power.[29] This political reality is reflected paradoxically in the running joke about Barnum in Manchester County that he is "*saved . . . from bein a nigger only by the color of his skin.*"[30] I emphasize *saved* here because the aim of the joke is to save or preserve the myth of white male supremacy. Barnum is raced as a white other because his poverty and behavior closely resemble the stereotyped and raced non-Europeans against which whiteness conceptually pits itself.

Revealing the tenacity of white supremacy, Jones shows that Barnum's white trash stigma intensifies his investment in white male supremacy even as he identifies on an emotional level with African American humanity and suffering. Barnum's chief white dilemma regarding his forced participation in selling Augustus is that he cannot productively reconcile his deep investment in white supremacy – and specifically white male privilege – with his moral imperative to treat African Americans humanely and his civic duty to uphold the rule of law that deems selling a free African American man back into slavery a crime. Barnum's "white trash" status intensifies the political and cultural stakes at play here because, on one side of the issue, upholding the "letter" of the law – as opposed to the white legal spirit of it – yields no productive benefit to his already "othered" white status. At best, he can expect to be labeled a "nigger-lover" by his white peers and cast further down the hierarchy of white male power. At worst, he can expect retaliation of a violent sort either from his co-conspirators in slave patrollers Harvey and Oden or from pro-slavery white men who might view him as a traitor for supporting an African American man over white-identified men.

On the other side of the issue, keeping the "crime" a secret and ignoring his moral imperative also come at a high emotional cost. They force Barnum, who is struggling to overcome alcoholism, to engage in the very types of unhealthy emotional denials that trigger and exacerbate his disease.

Tellingly, Jones identifies the source of Barnum's white dilemma when Barnum falls out of sobriety after being alcohol-free for months and confesses his crime to John Skiffington. Bemoaning his inability to reconcile the "twoness" of his gendered racial identity, Barnum babbles:

> There should be a way for a *body* to say what is without *somebody* sayin he standin on the nigger side. A *body* should be able to stand under some . . . kinda light and declare . . . "I know what I know and what I know is God's truth," and then come from under the light and *nobody* make any big commotion bout what he said. He could say it and just get on about his business, and *nobody* would say, "He be stickin up for the nigger, he be stickin up for them Indians." The lantern wouldn't low them to say that.[31]

Barnum's repeated use of the words "body," "nobody," and "somebody" draw attention directly to the source of his white dilemma. Beholden ideologically to the white, collective, social body, Barnum understands intuitively that he must accept that morality, ethics, and "god" are color-coded, that whites are naturally superior and African Americans naturally inferior. Predisposed by temperament to seeing the lie of this white discourse despite himself, Barnum becomes trapped, ideologically and emotionally, in his own white body. Jones illuminates this dynamic in Barnum's fanciful description of the ideal white existence. What Barnum longs for is an ideological social "body" free of racial prescriptions that would allow him to tell "God's truth," being in this case that the patroller Harvey was criminally wrong for selling Augustus Townsend, a free African American man, back into slavery, *without* being stripped of his white-male-body social privileges that give him power over African Americans, enslaved and free. Tellingly, he describes the imagined site of race-free morality as "being under the light"; the "light," in this instance, functioning not simply to illuminate the "truth" of the moral circumstance, but also to protect the truth-speaker from being stigmatized and cast out of the racial tribe. Barnum knows intuitively, as this scenario reveals, that he has to step out of the light and, consequently, back into moral darkness, to enjoy the real and imagined spoils of white supremacy.

Ultimately, Jones demonstrates in this scene that Barnum's moral crisis is largely, if not altogether consciously, self-imposed. Unwilling to challenge what W. E. B. Du Bois calls the "inherited customs" and "long established patterns of [racial] actions"[32] for fear of losing his claim to white supremacy, Barnum forecloses the possibility of reconciling his moral conflict. His desire for a mutable raced body that can be both morally upright and socially dominant cannot be fully actualized, because white supremacy depends parasitically on denying African American humanity. Barnum's unsuccessful attempts to overcome alcoholism, stay sober, and become a respectable and contributing member of white society reflect metaphorically the cost of seeing African American humanity in the antebellum South. The irony is that though Barnum is by all accounts the most morally awake white citizen in Manchester, he is, by virtue of his white trash status, the least likely person to be heard by his white peers. So when Barnum senses, for instance, that John Skiffington's cousin Counsel is lying about the circumstances surrounding John Skiffington's murder, the reader knows that nothing will come of it; even if Barnum chooses to speak out, as he does against Harvy and Oden, nobody will listen.

When we compare Barnum's experience of hegemonic white male power to that of William Robbins, which Jones clearly prompts us to do by reiterating that (in direct contrast to Barnum) Robbins is the richest man in Manchester County, we more clearly see the various levels of white power and how they radically inform and transform the experience of white supremacy. Though he, too, sees African American humanity and consistently breaks the customs and laws governing African American/white intimate relations, Robbins rarely questions the authenticity of his whiteness or agonizes over what others think about his actions (the lone exception being his relationship with his African American concubine, Philomena). Moreover, his social stature allows him to define the standards of whiteness and manhood and even to break the racial rules he establishes. In fact, he is able to sculpt his neurotic raced and classed views into law. Gripped with sellers' remorse several days after he sells two slaves for "well under market value" to a stranger who comes to his aid on the road one day when he is struck ill, Robbins decides that the stranger was a con man, an abolitionist in disguise, lying in wait for the opportunity to steal his property. He also decides that Sheriff Gilly Patterson is ultimately to blame for the breach and that the only way to keep this incident from escalating into a full-blown slave exodus or revolt is to create a slave patrol. When Patterson questions Robbins's rationale in a meeting with other prominent landowners, Robbins responds with a biting rhetorical question: "Gilly, how many slaves you got?"[33] Patterson returns, "None, William. You know that." Robbins then follows, "Well, Gilly, you don't know then. You don't know what the difficulty is in keeping this world going right. You ride around, keeping the peace, but that ain't got nothing to do with running a plantation fulla slaves."[34] Though Gilly later complains in private to then-deputy John Skiffington that he "ain't no fetch and carry,"[35] he internalizes his feelings in Robbins's presence and eventually caves to the bulk of Robbins's unwarranted demands.

Despite having a much stronger grip on reality than Robbins (the stranger was indeed a slave-trader and an opportunist), Patterson's perspective in this arena of wealth and power does not count. Even if Robbins knew, for instance, that Gilly disapproved of his "broad open daylight" cavorting "with a nigger and her children"[36] – and clearly Robbins anticipates this reaction when he builds Philomena a house "on the same block" in a white neighborhood – it would doubtless have little effect on his race/gender/class outlook. As we see in his cowering posture toward Robbins during the debate above, Gilly's whiteness and hegemonic white masculinity are thrown into crisis. Robbins's comments make Gilly feel like a "nigger child" and leave him "crippled" emotionally for years afterward.[37] Robbins's elite power status not only allows him to avoid the racial insecurities that plague Patterson and Barnum, but it empowers him to "race" and, in the case of Patterson, emasculate white men below him on the class and social scale.

Despite the power that he wields to define white manhood and, consequently, to dominate whites of lower class and social rank, Robbins is not completely insulated from suffering. The white and wealth privileges that allow Robbins to invent and police his version of reality are also the variables that blind him to patterns of self-sabotage in his most cherished relations. Consider his volatile relationship with Philomena, the person that he loves "far more than anything he could name."[38] Though Robbins desperately wants Philomena to love and desire him as much as he loves and desires her, because of his investment in gendered and classed white male supremacist ideology, he is unwilling to see her personhood beyond his desire and power. Robbins is accustomed to dominating everyone around him, including the overwhelming majority of whites. Because he cares deeply for Philomena, he tolerates from her rebellious behaviors that he will not stand for in most people, regardless of race.

A key problem for Robbins is that Philomena is not intimidated or impressed by his whiteness or social stature. Like Harriet Jacobs in *Incidents in the Life of a Slave Girl,* who approaches the inevitability of her sexual commodification as a business transaction and thus manages to exercise a modicum of control over her body and self-determination, Philomena turns an otherwise debilitating circumstance of forced concubinage to her advantage as well. She gets Robbins to legally free her (even if she is never truly free to leave), to allow her mother and brother to come live with her, and to acknowledge their children as his own in public. The crucial variable for Robbins, however, is that Philomena never feels dependent on what he gives her to make her happy. Hers is ultimately a desire for real freedom and self-determination. So, to truly make Philomena happy, Robbins has to free her unconditionally. Dominator that he is, Robbins never fully entertains this idea because, to his mind, the gifts and such that he gives Philomena, which by all counts are exorbitantly lavish by the social standards of the antebellum South, should be good enough to please a middle-class white woman, let alone an African American woman and former slave. Philomena's repeated and unsanctioned trips to Richmond, Virginia, then, are experienced by Robbins as an insult to his genuine efforts to please her. He is also disgusted with himself as a white man of wealth, prestige, and power because he has allowed himself to become emotionally vulnerable to an African American woman, the lowest of the socially low.

Little wonder that Robbins explodes into violence when he encounters her in Richmond. She refuses to heed his verbal demands that she return to Manchester and then physically and aggressively fights back when he tries to shake her into compliance. He is enraged with himself for needing her and enraged with her for *not* needing him. Rather than improve the chances that Philomena will grow to love him, Robbins's violence all but insures that the growing trust-breach between them will widen. When arranging to have Philomena stay on in Richmond for a few additional days to heal at the inn while he, Henry, and the children return to Manchester, Robbins thinks, "Even as they [the African American husband and wife innkeepers] all spoke and the man and the wife tried to assure him that they would bring Philomena to him, he began to fear that he would not see her again. He looked at her and could not take his eyes from her. He hoped that her love for their children would compel her back to Manchester. He dared not hope that any love for him would do it."[39] The irony here is unmistakable. Robbins fears that he will not see Philomena again because of his behavior when, in fact, his dilemma stems precisely from *not* seeing her in the first place. Wanting but not knowing how to love Philomena because of his investments in whiteness and hegemonic masculinity, Robbins, like Barnum and Clara, becomes his own worst enemy.

In Jones's rendering of Skiffington's tragic path toward self-destruction, the reader sees the political culmination of his warnings about the cost to white-identified people of internalized white supremacy. Though Skiffington believes his strong religious convictions set him apart morally from the slave-owning population and white men in particular, Jones demonstrates thematically throughout the novel that there is little, if any, substantive difference between Skiffington's practice of white hegemonic male power and that of his white male peers, including his cousin and murderer Counsel. Jones prompts the reader to see in Skiffington's specific negotiation of white hegemonic male power the extent to which whites generally, and white men in particular, devalue their white humanity beyond repair in their parasitical, unthought known relationships to African Americans. The toothache that dogs John in the final days of his life and his unsuccessful pursuit of a remedy from an African American slave woman root worker embody this idea in the novel. Read metaphorically, Skiffington's toothache constitutes his (dis)ease with dehumanizing raced others to secure white hegemonic male dominance. To enjoy his white hegemonic male dominance in good conscience, Skiffington must keep his white (dis)ease with power emotionally in check.

What this means for him specifically is getting African Americans to affirm his distorted notion of white moral superiority and to shoulder the emotional burden of his and whites' dehumanizing behavior toward them. This dynamic is reflected in Skiffington's inability to find a white dentist to help him. Indeed, he has cut himself off from his next-door neighbor, the only licensed dentist in the Manchester County, because he never owns up to allowing his dog to kill the dentist's chicken. The only other white person who can help him is the town undertaker, who happens to be out of town attending to family matters. The insertion of the undertaker in this scene clearly foreshadows Skiffington's demise – the causality of which is tied, on one level, to his willful blindness to the people he hurts and, on another, to the perverse white supremacist version of Christianity that he practices.

The nature of Skiffington's white (dis)ease, and the concomitant cost of his and white-identified groups' unthought known erasure of African American humanity, are visible in Skiffington's first encounter with the slave woman. The narrator reports that despite the fact that it is nearly dark outside and difficult to see, Skiffington does not "bother [to go] inside to where [the slave woman] lived" for her to examine his sore tooth under better lighting.[40] Skiffington's striking choice of words reveals another iteration of whites' gendered unthought known negotiation with African American humanity. To enjoy the social benefits of white hegemonic male power, Skiffington and white men have to remain consciously and unconsciously "in the dark" about African American humanity and pain. Because African American women *as* women were in many ways the most vulnerable and least threatening group – besides children – to white men during slavery, Jones's decision to put Skiffington at the medical mercy of an African American woman he cannot see appears hardly coincidental. Indeed, the novel reveals that during the time John is meeting with the slave woman, he is mulling over a decision to rape his lone slave and pretend-daughter Minerva. Viewing access to African American women's bodies as a white male entitlement and African American women as willing sexual participants, Skiffington never considers Minerva's feelings in his internal deliberations over raping her. His only real concerns are that his actions may create friction in his marriage and possibly taint his public persona as a religiously devout man.

Racialized gender issues aside, the most pressing danger that Skiffington and other whites face for not seeing African American humanity
and pain is the social, cultural, and economic devaluation of white humanity. The crucial point here is that humanity as such does not abide
by social constructions of whiteness and race. As Morrison avers, the
"very concept of whiteness ... [is] an inhuman idea"[41] that "dismembers"
white-identified groups from their familial "place as ... human[s] in the
world."[42] She asserts further that whiteness and racism are antithetical to
emotional health and well-being. Those who embrace them rupture ties
with humanity at large and undergo "severe fragmentation of the self."[43]

Read through this critical lens, the pain and human complexity that
Skiffington, as a white-identified man, orchestrates not to see or comprehend in the slave woman and African Americans' lives directly retard
his ability to see and comprehend his own human pain and complexity
and that of his white-identified peers. Skiffington's multiple misreadings
of the slave woman's advice about how to fix his toothache bring the
problems of white impaired sight and comprehension into clearer focus.
When, for instance, she tells Skiffington that the only way to end his
white pain is for *him* to pull the tooth out "by the root and ... till there
ain't nothing left," he misinterprets her directive as an offer to extract
the tooth for him.[44] Even after she clarifies her position, that he must
perform the extraction himself, he comes back the next day with an of-
fering of a fifty-cent piece, a hefty sum to give a slave regardless of the
circumstance, misreading her initial refusal as a ploy to insure payment.
The slave woman is trying to buy her way out of slavery and is logistically
not in a financial position to turn down such a lucrative offer, as she has
only amassed $113 of the $350 her master demands for her freedom. That
she declines Skiffington's offer *despite* her financial predicament highlights the gross inadequacy of Skiffington's "payoff" for African American erasure. The slave woman reflects this thinking in her explanation:
"You got a back ache, you got a heart ache, you got a foot ache, I can help
you. But I don't like to go to the mouth. Too far away from what I know
bout helpin [white] people. Too near the [white] brain."[45] Couched in
the slave woman's cleverly worded explanation is a rather humorous jab
at Skiffington's bankrupt white capitalistic gesture and lack of (in)sight.
Her assertion that she avoids operating on the mouth because it is "too

near the [white] brain" suggests that Skiffington's investment in white supremacy has caused a form of "brain" damage for which there is no viable cure – at least not one that she is *willing* as a raced other to provide. In listing off her fields of "medical" expertise, none of which have anything to do with healing the mind, the slave woman is basically washing her hands of whites' perversities and putting the onus back on Skiffington and whites to own the burden of white supremacy and the dehumanizing of African Americans. Her parting words to Skiffington that she "might hurt" him more than "help him" if she "touched" his mouth underscores this mindset, revealing paradoxically that to "help" Skiffington and white men avoid having to give an account for their oppressive behavior is to reinforce the status quo and become complicit in white oppression.

Because he cannot see the slave woman beyond her prescribed subordinate social status, Skiffington misses the lesson in her refusal to operate on his mouth. In a real and symbolic way, his inability to see or hear her leads directly to his death. Like the diseased tooth that he never pulls out, Skiffington keeps his investment in whiteness painfully intact. As such, he fails to see that the true threat to his physical safety is not the runaway slave Moses, whom he hunts down to Mildred's house, but a family member and fellow police officer, Counsel, whose job it is to watch his back. Jones hammers home politically, in John Skiffington's distorted white vision and brutal murder, that the parasitical nature of white freedom extends beyond the erasure of African American humanity. To justify murdering Skiffington and reclaiming his lost wealth, Counsel appropriates a version of the Judeo-Christian doctrine that Skiffington uses to justify his sexual claim over Minerva's body and to explain away his responsibility for killing Henry's mother Mildred. Functioning as the "official" marker or history of the calamity will be none other than the tombstone that Counsel envisions erecting with the money he steals from the Townsends and kills Skiffington over, a tombstone so ostentatious in size and appearance that "wild and insane men would come down from their lairs in the Virginia mountains" to worship it.[46] Jones's signifying cultural gesture is not subtle. The insanity of white supremacist thinking begets further insanity.

Jones best captures this white supremacist insanity as it applies to African American slave-owners by repeatedly exploding the links

between racial subjectivity and critical insight. In particular, he demonstrates that their claims to higher moral and ethical grounds on the
basis of their status as former slaves and/or victims of white supremacist
domination are but an extension of white supremacist slavery ideology.
This political trajectory allows us to see that Henry Townsend's quest to
be "a better master than any white man he had ever known" is politically
naive at best and willfully delusional at worst – namely, because such
mastery is inextricably tied to erasing the humanity of the enslaved.[47]
Morally speaking, Henry's goal to be a better, more humane master is
thus already bankrupt. Jones's narrator reflects this political sentiment
in the novel, observing that Henry "did not understand that the kind of
world he wanted to create was doomed before he had even spoken the
first syllable of the word *master*."[48]

The reader witnesses the futility of Henry's goal to best his white
peers as masters in the scene where his mentor and surrogate father-
figure, William Robbins, catches him playfully wrestling with his first
slave, Moses. Pulling Henry to the side, Robbins admonishes him not to
blur the lines of power between master and slave. He warns that doing so
undermines the law that protects him as a master and compromises the
unspoken "bargain" of wielding power and authority over the enslaved.
Robbins expounds, "You will have pointed to the line that separates
you from your property and told your property that the line does not
matter."[49] What stands out here and speaks to the inherent pathology of
white supremacist logic is that Robbins has transgressed every master/
slavery boundary that he warns Henry against, including blurring the
master/slave lines in his relationship with Philomena and compromising
the authority of the very law enforcement agency he essentially bank-
rolls. Henry, who has witnessed and helped facilitate many of Robbins's
transgressions, fully embraces his mentor's advice and begins forthwith
to physically and verbally attack Moses on trumped-up claims of insub-
ordination. Jones reveals the moral consequences of Henry's "bargain"
with Robbins and white supremacist slavery by creating an afterlife that
has Henry enclosed claustrophobically in a miniature house, a far cry
from the mansion he had envisioned as his rightful spiritual resting place
for being a "good" master.

An examination of the exploitative, sexual relationship that develops between Caldonia, Henry's wife, and the slave Moses reveals additional ways in which white supremacist models of domination bankrupt the moral claims and critical insights of the African American elite. Caldonia's sexual relationship with Moses is sparked on the one hand by her need to memorialize her husband as a good slave master, and, on the other, it is a way to reconcile her (im)moral decision not to free her slaves after his death. Little wonder, then, that the sexual/emotional catalyst for the relationship is Moses's elaborate fabrications about Henry as a loving master and husband. Like many of her white slaveholding peers, Caldonia depends emotionally on her slaves' complicity in white supremacist slavery ideology to stave off the bloody reality of her oppressive enterprise. The "success" of such unthought known negotiations hinges on conditioned evasiveness. Caldonia's identification with this gendered white supremacist mindset plays out in the way she views her sexual relations with Moses as "a kind of miscegenation" and becomes preoccupied, like Clara becomes regarding Ralph, with the social scandal of being found out. Though the sociopolitical stakes for Caldonia and Clara certainly differ in scope because Clara is white, Caldonia's negotiation of her unthought known erasure of Moses's humanity is no less parasitical than Clara's erasure of Ralph's. While Caldonia does not put Moses directly in the line of white fire, as Clara does Ralph, she ignites his emotional collapse and eventual white torture by parasitically ignoring his personhood and stakes in the relationship. This pattern of unthought known behavior is reflected in the salient disconnect between her claims to love Moses and her unwillingness to set him free. Moreover, it becomes apparent in her sudden epiphany, after Sheriff Skiffington suggests that Moses may be tied to the disappearance of his wife and son and the slave Alice, that "she had been making love to another woman's husband."[50]

Though Moses is certainly complicit to a degree in reinforcing Caldonia's white supremacist perversities and power negotiations (he clearly aspires to marry Caldonia and take Henry's place as the new slave master), his complicity is driven by a different social apparatus. Like Lorraine, who becomes Caldonia's bodyguard, and Elias, who assists white

police in hunting down Moses, Moses's complicity reflects how pro-
longed exposure to, and brutalization under, white supremacist slavery
regimes corrupts the cultural and moral consciousness of the enslaved.
We see the trajectory of Moses's unique corruption in the striking difference in his temperament and moral consciousness before and after
Henry purchases him. In the brief jail sequence in the novel, Jones offers
us an endearing, if heartbreaking, portrait of Moses as he pleads desperately with Robbins (who makes the purchase on Henry's behalf) not to
separate him from his crippled love interest Bessie: "She all I have in the
world. We is one as a family."⁵¹ Moses's requests fall on deaf ears and he is
forever separated from Bessie. Hardened emotionally by this and similar
dehumanizing gestures, Moses – like the slave Ella in Toni Morrison's
Beloved – learns to "don't love nothing."⁵² We see this mindset play out in
Moses's emotionally strained and physically abusive relationships with
his wife and son and, concomitantly, in how easily he dispenses with
them (albeit by helping them escape) when he thinks Caldonia is going
to set him free and marry him.

Similar to sufferers of battered person's syndrome, Moses's feelings
of despair and helplessness toward the institutions and people that oppress him compel him to identify with the oppressor rather than the
oppressed. Indeed, he heaps the bulk of his furor on slaves who, like
Elias, actively challenge white supremacy and slavery. Jones registers
Moses's skewed moral and ideological compass in his botched escape
attempt. "World-stupid" and directionally challenged, Moses runs south
toward slavery instead of north away from it. Though clearly not letting
Moses off the hook for his gender abuses and willful complicity in white
supremacist slavery, Jones prompts the reader to empathize with Moses
as a tragic victim of abuse. A case in point is the climactic capture scene
where Jones offers a strikingly redemptive portrait of Moses as he at-
tends to Mildred's slain body under white gunpoint. Moses's tenderness
toward Mildred, for whom he struggles emotionally to find the proper
words of thanks, recalls his raw affection toward Bessie and his openness
to emotional attachment before becoming Henry's slave. The narrator
reports, "He knew he was grateful to her and so as he worked [to put her
body on the table] he thanked Mildred for helping him . . . and closed
[her] eyes."⁵³ Although Moses's complicity in oppression is reprehen-

sible, the bigger tragedy is the white supremacist slavery experiences that have brought Moses and the enslaved so low.

Jones's most profound engagement with white supremacist ideology, slavery, and African American consciousness involves slave-owner Fern Elston and runaway slave Jebediah Dickinson. Even as she identifies as black despite having light enough skin to pass as white, Fern is an avid, if conflicted, colorist who evaluates intellect, morality, and personhood via a white supremacist ideological lens. Her colorist notions about Africans are, indeed, a key component to her vision of herself as a paternalistic and morally just master. Parodying this mindset, Jones's narrator relates that Fern "didn't have slaves, colored people said, [she] had neighbors who happened to be slaves."[54] Given Fern's white skin and colorist notions, it is hardly a coincidence that Jones creates a dark-skinned, fearless, intellectually sharp, and fully self-actualized character like Jebediah to expose the crisis of her investment in white supremacist ideology. With his striking Afrocentric features, slave vernacular, and generally "uncultured" ways, Jebediah is precisely the kind of enslaved African who makes Fern feel racially superior and justified socially in owning slaves. Jebediah thrusts Fern into a state of ideological crisis, defying both her colorist expectations of racial inferiority and openly refusing to abide by socially mandated master/slave rules of engagement. Though "it had never crossed Fern's mind to pass as white" because she did not "care very much for white people,"[55] we see the depths of her dependency on white supremacist ideology in her repeated attempts to beat Jedediah into compliance and silence his truth-telling. Most unsettling for Fern are Jebediah's responses to her white supremacist slave mindset as inherently pathological. Her assertion, relayed in the company of her African American slave-owning peers, that Jebediah makes her feel "like I belong to him, that I am his property," reflects this phenomenon.[56] We can read Fern's decision to free Jebediah shortly after his accident and foot amputation as an attempt to rid herself of his critical gaze. Freeing him fails to do the trick, however, because Jebediah comprehends the moral bankruptcy of the gesture, including the emotional capital of gifting freedom that Fern expects in return.[57] Jones dramatizes this comprehension when Jebediah flippantly hands his free papers back to Fern, noting a key spelling error and reflecting his grammatical mastery of the English language: "Ain't but one 'T' in manumit . . . cept when you usin the pas tense."[58]

The tragicomic joke here is on Fern. Despite being a lauded teacher and moralist, she does not know the proper spelling or grammatical usage of a word that means, "to set free from slavery." What becomes clear to the reader (and Fern) is that Jebediah is better equipped intellectually and morally to script his own path to freedom. In actuality, Fern is indebted to Jebediah. She is also the true (ideological) slave. The novel drives these political messages home in Jebediah's parting words to Fern after she gives him a horse, a wagon, and fifty dollars to see him off: "You and your no-good husband owe me $450 more and there ain't no way round it. I give yall the work I done and my foot for free."[59] Jebediah's indictment not only illuminates the insufficiency of Fern's fifty-dollar payoff to clear the gambling debt owed him, but the more egregious theft of his labor, limb, and humanity to slavery. Indeed, his sardonic assertion that he will "give" the Elstons "the work I done and my foot for free" reverses the gifting-of-freedom formulation within white supremacist slavery ideology that allows Fern and slave-owners to gain emotional capital from exploiting the enslaved. As someone holding a deep respect for African American men who are fearless to the point of death about their ethical convictions, especially as it concerns standing up to oppressive white men, Fern admires Jebediah's stance despite herself. To ease her conscience, she makes a personal vow to pay him the debt in full if she ever hears from him again. That she is ultimately unable to pay off the debt (she never hears from Jebediah again) forever riddles her with guilt and reflects, metaphorically, the permanent damage that white supremacist slavery leaves in its wake.

Jones maps a path of growth beyond white supremacist ideology for a few of the African American slave-owners,[60] including Fern, who later remarries and has two children with a "pecan-colored" former slave. Fern also realizes several years after Jebediah's departure that she was intensely attracted to him; she even contemplates a married life with him. In stark contrast, Jones provides no such trajectory for any of the white-identified characters in the novel. While it is tempting to see this disparity in treatment as a nod to African Americans' greater capacity for growth, a more plausible explanation is that he wants to reflect that whites have a deeper and, in some ways, more cancerous investment in white supremacist ideology. Jones's delineation of this reality in *The Known World* prompts readers to see white slave-owners as a tragic, if contemptible, lot. If we reserve more empathy toward the African American slave-owners, it is perhaps because we expect better from those who have suffered most. What Jones provides is not so much a challenge to this expectation – for Jones clearly expects better of African Americans on this score – but a hard dose of reality regarding African Americans' conscious and unconscious collusion with whites in slavery, white supremacist ideology, and self-sabotage. Painful though it may be to contemplate this unflattering side of African American consciousness, it is a crucial part of our story – a story that, to invoke Morrison's narrator in *Beloved*, we cannot afford "to pass on."[61]

The master's tools will never dismantle the master's house.

Audre Lorde, *Sister Outsider: Essays and Speeches*

Why? Why? Why? Why? Why?

Paul D in Toni Morrison's *Beloved*

TWO

Easier Said Than Done: Making Black Feminism Transformative for Black Men

A CURIOUS THING HAPPENS IN TONI MORRISON'S *BELOVED* when Stamp Paid and Paul D are conversing outside of a makeshift church about Paul D's breakup with Sethe. As the reader will recall, Stamp Paid has facilitated this breakup in the name of protecting Paul D by proffering him information about Sethe's infanticide and criminal proceedings. Having reflected upon his actions and witnessed the harm he has caused Sethe and Paul D alike, Stamp Paid tries to rectify his meddling by apologizing to both. He seeks out Sethe first, but intense feelings of shame, guilt, and gendered entitlement ultimately stall his apology attempt. The scene in question occurs after his multiple failed attempts to approach Sethe. In seeking out Paul D, Stamp Paid learns that he is sleeping in the cold cellar of a makeshift church. Stamp Paid is appalled, believing (wrongly) that the town, out of spite for his relationship with Sethe, has turned on Paul D and refused to house him. While the two men are engaged in an intense discussion about this misunderstanding and the circumstances of Stamp Paid's intervention into Paul D's relationship with Sethe, an unidentified man rides into town on horseback and abruptly interrupts their conversation. Dispensing with formalities, he simply says, "Hey," to get the men's attention and then asks them if they know "a gal name of Judy" who lives on Plank Road.[1] Though Morrison does not reveal the man's race, the reader intuits that he is white by the ways in which he interacts with Stamp Paid and Paul D. Stamp Paid's marked shift in diction and behavior confirms this reality. Instead of taking offense at the white man's brassy interruption, Stamp Paid responds with servility, asking, "Yes, sir?" Further, he prevaricates and says that he does not know Judy but can gladly offer directions to Plank Road. The tension lingering in the air is that the man is in town slumming. Metaphorically speaking, he embodies the unspeakable, coercive, dominant white male power against which Stamp Paid, Paul D, and black men's masculinity is socially pitted and measured. That the white man feels completely comfortable, if not entitled, in slumming for sex in the black town is particularly striking, for it draws attention thematically to Stamp Paid and Paul D's social impotence as "real men," especially in regard to protecting and upholding the honor of black women. We also see the pernicious reach and effect of white male surveillance on black male consciousness. Morrison registers the intensity of this phenomenon for black men in how the white man responds to Paul D (who is openly drinking whiskey on the church steps) after Stamp Paid gives him directions. The white man trots off a bit but then turns around and launches a threat: "Look here . . . There's a cross up there, so I guess this here's a church or used to be. Seems to me like you ought to show it some respect, you follow me?"[2]

Though we are not privy to what Paul D is doing when Stamp Paid first talks to the white man – which is, no doubt, also an intentional move on Morrison's part[3] – we can deduce from the white man's warning that he is threatened by Paul D's body language or gaze. Indeed, the wicked hypocrisy of the white man's moral outrage in the name of white Christian morality (his sole purpose for being in an all-black space is debauchery) illuminates the twisted moral double standard upon which gendered white superiority rests. Paul D's true transgression is not that he is drinking whiskey in front of a church, but that he refuses in some bodily way to accommodate the white man's sense of moral superiority and white male entitlement. Acutely aware of what the white man *truly* wants and the dangers involved in not giving it to him, Stamp Paid intervenes: "Yes, sir . . . You right about that. That's just what I come over to talk to him about. Just that."[4]

Even though we have only Stamp Paid's comments at our disposal, we know that the white rider ultimately receives the response of deference he seeks from both men because he rides away without violence or further comment. While Stamp Paid's performance of gendered servility successfully pacifies the white rider and perhaps even saves Paul D's life, it also reflects the social and political impotence of black men at the time. We know that both men are conscious of this dynamic by the ways in which their conversation shifts after the white rider leaves. Stamp Paid's coping mechanism is clear. He pretends nothing of import occurred and picks up where he left off in conversation before the white man interrupted them – namely, he reassures Paul D that he is welcome to bunk anywhere in town that he sees fit. Clearly at his wit's end with white male power and moral hypocrisy, Paul D redirects the conversation back to what transpired between them and the white man on horseback:

> "What about Judy? She take me in?"
>
> "Depends. What you got in mind?"
>
> "You know Judy?
>
> "Judith. I know everybody."
>
> "Out on Plank Road?"
>
> "Everybody."
>
> "Well? She take me in?"[5]

Paul D's fixation on Judy/Judith bespeaks his frustration with Stamp Paid, himself, and black men for cowering time and again to white male authority and power. What Paul D understands, at least intuitively, is that white male power is tied to the ability to control and dominate black bodies across gender lines. His mock request to stay with Judy/Judith underscores his anger at Stamp Paid and himself for being unable to stand up against white male power and sexual exploitation of black women. It also calls our attention to the limitations of his gendered oppositional mindset – he thinks about defying white male power in myopic patriarchal terms. Control over Judy and black women's bodies – not exploding (white) patriarchy – emerges as the pressing issue at hand. The challenge before Paul D (a white rape survivor himself) and black men is that they do not possess a critical language or discourse to think through their anger, frustration, fear, vulnerability, and empowerment as gendered, sexualized, and racial subjects. As white middle-class male hegemony during slavery defined masculinity in terms of socioeconomic power and dominance over the bodies of blacks and white women, the gendered oppositional response of black men was predictably to treat the white men who wielded the power, rather than the system of white male dominance itself, as the culprit of black emasculation. Paul D and Stamp Paid epitomize this dynamic. However, rather than condemn Paul D, Stamp Paid, and black men for their gendered blindness and complicity in white male supremacy in *Beloved*, Morrison usefully highlights the real and complicated obstacles, such as white male surveillance and internalized status quo patriarchy, that frustrate the development of a critical nonhierarchal and anti-sexist black masculine discourse. Indeed, Morrison approaches black male accountability as it concerns reinforcing white male supremacy and subjugating black women as an organically complex and confounding issue – complex and confounding, that is, precisely because of the untold scars of black oppression across gender lines and the unspeakable pathology of white male supremacy that we discussed in chapter 1.

I open chapter 2 with a discussion of this oft-overlooked moment in Toni Morrison's *Beloved* because I want to think critically here about the social and material stakes involved for black men today in rethinking gender/race/class politics through a black feminist political lens. Even as she captures the enduring resilience of black folk, Morrison actively resists romanticizing the complex process of healing and understanding across and within black gender lines. Her emphasis on black women's experiences of suffering under slavery is designed not to attack black men, but rather to call attention to the ways that the discourse of black suffering is gendered male. Making black women's unique experiences of oppression visible in this discourse allows us to see the ways that the intersectionality of subjectivity plays out in cultural space and lived experience. It also helps us to think critically about why black men negotiate their agency as men against and through white patriarchal models of manhood and social power. What becomes clear on one level is that the attraction/repulsion that black men have toward white hegemonic masculinity wreaks emotional havoc on black men's relationships with *each other* and with black women.

In this chapter I strive to develop a critical discourse to think about the challenges and obstacles to convincing black men generally and heteronormative black men in particular to embrace black feminism[6] or, at the very least, the revolutionary notions of empowerment and resistance therein.[7] While I have traditionally shied away from personal disclosure in my scholarship, in part because I'm a private person and in part because such disclosure – however well-intended – can wind up being politically self-serving, I think the kind of personal-political intervention that I am advocating for in this chapter demands that I do so. Michael Awkward's insights on self-disclosure as a black man in feminism informs my thinking here and are worth revisiting. In *Negotiating Difference: Race, Gender, and the Politics of Positionality* (1995), Michael Awkward thinks through his participation in black feminist discourse via Hortense Spillers's formulation of black men's "debilitating split" subjectivity in "Mama's Baby, Papa's Maybe." According to Awkward, black men in Spillers's formulation emerge as split subjects because, as the only male community in the United States to be separated from "paternal name and law," they are – and have been – pressed out of necessity to "learn *who* the female is within the self."[8] While admiring of Spillers's formulation (particularly because she thinks critically about black men's unique positionality as gendered and raced subjects vis-à-vis black women and within white male supremacy), Awkward argues that his participation in black feminism arose not from this debilitating split subjectivity, but rather from identifying with his mother's plight as an abused woman and from wishing not to reproduce the modalities of black masculinity that sanctioned such abuse. He recalls that his mother perpetually warned him not to "grow up to be like your father" – a father who, she told him, kicked her "in the stomach when my fetal presence swelled her body, because he believed she'd been unfaithful to him and that I was only 'maybe' his baby."[9] Awkward elaborates:

> As a youth, I pondered this and other such stories often and deeply, in part because of the pain I knew these incidences caused my mother, in part because, as someone without a consistent male familial role model, I actively sought a way to achieve a gendered self-definition. As one for whom maleness as manifested in the way surrounding inner city culture seemed to be represented only by violence, familial abandonment, and the certainty of imprisonment, I found that I was able to define myself with regard to my gender primarily in oppositional ways. I had internalized the cautionary intent of my mother's narratives, which also served as her dearest wish for me: that I not grow up to be like my father, that I not adopt the definitions of "maleness" represented by his example and the culture generally. Because the scars of male brutality were visibly etched – literally marked, as it were – on my mother's flesh and on her psyche, "maleness,"

as figured both in her stories and in my environment, seemed to me not to be a
viable mimetic option. I grew up, then, not always sure of what or who I was with
respect to prevailing social definitions of gender but generally quite painfully
aware of what I could not become.[10]

Awkward explains that even as he identified with his mother and
rejected the modalities of black manhood available to him, he lacked a
critical discourse at the time to think about the possibilities and contours
of alternative masculinities. He opines that his introduction to African
American literature as a sophomore in college helped him to comprehend "aspects of my mother's life" and get a grasp on "what a man against
patriarchy could be and do."[11] He was drawn to black women's literature
and, by extension, black feminist criticism because they provided him
with "answers" about patriarchy and black womanhood that were not
available anywhere else. He explains, "I write and read what and as I do
because I am incapable of escaping the meanings of my mother's narratives for my own life." He notes further that black women's literature
"has given me parts of myself that – incapable of a (biological) 'fatherly
reprieve' – I would not otherwise have." He concludes that whether or
not his participation in black feminism "permits me to call myself 'feminist'" is ultimately "irrelevant": "What is most important to me is that
my work contribute, in however small a way, to the project whose goal
is the dismantling of the phallocentric rule by which black females and,
I am sure, countless other Afro-American sons have been injuriously
'touched.'"[12]

Like Awkward, my path to black feminism came through my engagement with African American women's writing. Unlike Awkward,
however, I was reared in a socially and religiously conservative, two-
parent, working-class home. In my house, my father had the first and last
word. If I struggled with my masculine identity, it was partly because
I wanted to please my father – a leader who was highly respected and
admired in my local neighborhood, church, and community at large. To
be sure, I wanted to grow up to be the kind of man that would make him
proud. Despite my admiration for my father, I was deeply troubled by his
treatment of my mother and women. My world was turned upside down
when I was a preteen and learned that my maternal aunt – who came to
live with us when she was eight years old after my grandparents died – be-

came pregnant at sixteen with my father's child. The official narrative in my family – supported and, indeed, policed by my mother – was that my aunt was a homewrecker, that she was "fast" and betrayed my mother by coming into our house and seducing my father. If my father was at fault at all, it was because he had let his guard down and allowed himself to be seduced. All was (provisionally) forgiven, though not forgotten, by my mother, because my father had "repented" at the church and agreed not to have any contact with my aunt or, as it turns out, my othered sister that resulted from the pregnancy. Because the community at large stigmatized my aunt and rallied around my father (who for many was the true victim) and, to a lesser degree, my mother (who gained social capital for standing by her man), I had no viable gendered discourse at the time to work through my conflicted feelings about my parents' (patriarchal) failings and my aunt's sexual abuse.

It wasn't until I was twenty-five, married, and a graduate student that I was introduced to black feminism and began thinking critically about the black patriarchal narrative that I had internalized. Though there were many moments of revelation throughout my process of coming to grips with who my father really was and how, as a man, I fit into the matrix of black patriarchal power, one moment in particular stands out. Though I had known that the so-called sexual relationship between my father and aunt had started when she was only eight years old, I was so conditioned by my environment "not to see" my father and "respectable" black men of his stature as victimizers, that I genuinely did not see the perversity of it all. That is, not until I was discussing the matter with my then partner-wife – a black feminist scholar – while driving to the grocery store one cool autumn day in Madison, Wisconsin. Her exact words were: "David, I understand that you love and respect your father, but what do you call a grown man that has sex with an eight-year-old girl?" I answered: "A pedophile." As the words left my lips I felt sickened and angry. Sickened and angry not only at my father's actions, but at my unconscious complicity in defending the patriarchal narrative that provided him with cultural and political cover – complicity that also included distancing myself from my aunt and her child (my othered sister) out of respect for my mother, who experienced her sister's sexual molestation as an unforgivable act of familial betrayal.

To further complicate matters, my mother, by all accounts, was one
of the most feminist-minded folks in my family, and I (the eldest son of
five children) was the metaphoric apple of her eye. Indeed, the bulk of the
women in my family were "womanish," to borrow Alice Walker's term,
when it came to dealing with men and patriarchy.[13] My mother was not
only womanish in her dealing with my father and black men, but she was
also womanish in her dealings with white men. As a youth, I watched
with deep admiration as she out-talked, outsmarted, and outmaneu-
vered white male superintendents, principals, teachers, and policemen
alike in the small Southern town of my upbringing. Moreover, in my
household, there was virtually no such thing as woman's work, at least
not when it came to chores we were assigned as kids. All my mother's
children (three boys and two girls) washed clothes, cooked, cleaned,
cut grass, chopped wood, went fishing, and changed the oil in their cars.
Though poverty and social circumstance prevented her from pursuing a
college degree, my mother was an organically brilliant woman with an
acute and unflinching sense of social justice. Though I had no discourse
to give voice to it at the time, her black feminist sensibilities, much more
than my father's patriarchal ones, are what ultimately shaped my notions
of what it meant to be a real man. The rub was that my mother's feminist
sensibilities did not fully extend to black men that she loved or deemed
respectable, including her sons, her brothers, and, most especially, her
husband. This painful reality was brought radically into focus when I
sought out my aunt and othered sister to apologize on behalf of the family and set the record straight about my aunt's sexual molestation. When
my father tried to intimidate me into silence by threats of armed retaliation, my mother dutifully backed him. Moreover, the other women in
my immediate and nuclear family, including my other two sisters, rushed
to my father's defense. My brothers remained silent, aware of the truth
of my claims but unwilling to challenge my father's authority. In the
end, I was framed as a troublemaker who was not only disrespecting
my father – who had repented of his sins (read: infidelity) before the
church, God, and his community – but also my mother, whose only fault,
it seemed, was loving and trusting her baby sister.[14]

At the height of this familial fallout, it just so happened that I was
in the midst of writing my dissertation on the role of black men in black

feminist studies. When I shared my familial challenges with my mentor – the late Nellie McKay – she encouraged me to explore the political implications of my experience in my intellectual engagement with black feminist theorizing. She even introduced me to Toni Cade Bambara's *The Salt Eaters* and Walter Mosley's collection of short stories, *Always Outnumbered, Always Outgunned,* remarking simply, "I think this is what you are doing." Though in the moment I didn't exactly know what "this" was or, for that matter, whether I had anything of significance to add to the discourse at all, Professor McKay seemed to have no doubts. Indeed, had it not been for her encouragement and guidance, I would never have considered writing a dissertation and then a book on black feminism and the issue of complicity in oppression across gender lines. My first book, *Breaking the Silence: Toward a Black Male Feminist Criticism,* then, was far more than an intellectual enterprise; it was an earnest, if ultimately flawed and incomplete, effort to illuminate how black patriarchal appeals to victimization, racial solidarity, and community empowerment were counterrevolutionary, rendering patriarchal black men, and the black women who support them, complicit in white male supremacy.

It is important to note that my feminist-inspired challenges to my father's authority and to the patriarchal narrative that erased my aunt's sexual abuse were ultimately not in vain. Since my intervention, my othered sister, now married with two children, has developed strong ties with all of her siblings, including myself. The intervention has also opened the door for my othered sister to have a relationship with my father, which she had desperately longed for throughout her childhood. My aunt is even provisionally welcomed at my parents' house now. And though my aunt and I have never spoken openly about the circumstances of her abuse, she walked up to me and grasped my hand tightly during my othered sister's high school graduation – which occurred only eight months after my intervention – and said, "I got the letters. They meant a lot. Thank you."[15] As for my father (a deacon in his longtime church), he remains shielded from owning up to his abuses of power and gender privilege. Indeed, my challenges to my father's patriarchal rule that prompted threats of violence and social ostracism have entered the cultural domain of the unspeakable in my nuclear family. The familial party line is, as the colloquialism goes, to "let sleeping dogs lie." From the outside looking in, we probably appear to be a tight-knit family. Truth is, however, the scars run deep; and though my aunt and othered sisters are now a visible part of the family, the patriarchal narrative that erases my aunt's sexual molestation at the hands of my father remains tenaciously intact. The enabling, patriarchy-driven climate means that the potential for a repeat offense are quite high. Given that I have young children of my own, I can't afford to be blind or enabling. To subscribe to the familial thinking that governs my family and community's lofty view of my father is to put my children's health and well-being at risk.

Even though I am cognizant of the patriarchal pressures to conform and the importance of breaking the silence on such issues of abuse, as I write this essay I can't help but feel that I am somehow betraying my father and my family. The reality is that such patriarchal pressure to fall in line is exactly what sustains such dangerous discourses and gives cultural license to the kind of abuse – sexual and otherwise – that has scarred my family. Even as I cannot deny the important contributions that my father has made in my life (and there are certainly many) and in those of others, I also cannot deny that his abuses of power and authority have wounded just as many lives, most especially my aunt's. Loving my father, then, does not require excusing his faults or keeping his secrets. Indeed, to love him in this instance means holding him and, by extension, those who uncritically support him, accountable for enabling and perpetuating his destructive patriarchal behavior. That said, I have no desire to sever ties with my father or my family; they have been – and are – some of my strongest supporters. And though my father continues to experience his sexual molestation toward my aunt as an ill-advised sexual affair between consenting adults, my refusal to cosign his vantage point even for the sake of family peace has at the very least disrupted the "unthought known" rewriting of sexual abuse in my family.

My familial obstacles and near-violent run-ins with my father have helped me to see the dangers of internalizing patriarchal thinking for black men. I have no doubt that my father *genuinely* experiences his crimes and abuses as minor and sees my challenges to them as unfounded and irresponsible. I'm reminded here of Jody Starks's response of patriarchal indignation on his deathbed toward Janie in Zora Neale Hurston's *Their Eyes Were Watching God*. Having so deeply internalized (middle-classed) patriarchy, he misreads Janie's self-defensive response to his verbal assaults and attempts to silence her throughout their marriage as a deliberate and calculated act of betrayal. Because he cannot see Janie or the legitimacy of her self-defensive response to patriarchy, he cannot fully appreciate her intelligence or insights. Indeed, his blindness literally costs him his life, for as the reader learns, if Jody had listened to Janie's advice and sought out a doctor when he first became ill, he would likely have survived. The truth is, a version of the patriarchal blindness that allows Jody and my father to excuse and/or explain away their abuses toward women is operational for all men. The pressing question, then, is not *whether* black men, myself included, are prone to exploit patriarchal privilege (however provisional that privilege may be in any given moment or social context), but rather how do black men, and I, resist the inevitably of that privilege and the gendered blindness that it fosters. Like Jody in *Their Eyes,* black men ignore this pressing question at our own peril.

To move toward resolution on this daunting question, we must first contextualize the problem. It is not mere happenstance that black men embrace status quo masculinity. As Patricia Hill Collins explains, "Because the racial normality attributed to whites has been defined in gender-specific terms, African American progress, or lack thereof, in achieving white gender norms has long been used as a marker of racial progress and has often been used to explain and to justify racial inequality itself."[16] Hill Collins expounds that two "commonsense" understandings about black manhood have framed how black men see their race-gender-class agency in the public domain. The first understanding is that black men's failings as men are attributable to women being too strong and men too weak. The second understanding pits black men against white men in terms of dominance and control. As notions of normative masculinity are bound up with dominating women and weaker men, and as they extend "to exclusive control over the economic, political, and social order," white men – who ultimately define the terms upon which this gendered normativity rests – emerge as strong men, while black men, by comparison, emerge as weak and deviant. In the former commonsense understanding of black manhood, black women emerge as the enemy, inasmuch as they are perceived as an emasculating force for "failing" to submit to subordinate gender status. Black men thus see themselves as victims, of a sort, in relation to so-called domineering black women. As being a real man rests, in part, on demonstrating to other men that you have control and dominance over such black women, black men who appear not to exercise that control are labeled by other men as weak.[17]

In the latter commonsense understanding of manhood, because the socioeconomic deck of power, so to speak, is heavily stacked against them, black men appear perpetually weak. Hill Collins explains,

> Using white masculinity as a yardstick for a normal masculinity grounded in ideas about strength as dominance, African American men become defined as subordinates, deviant, and allegedly weak, and black men's purported weakness as men is compared to the seeming strength of white men. Despite a complicated reality that structurally subordinates both black men and black women to white men, black men's subordination nevertheless becomes ideologically defined as a weakness in relation to both black women and white men.[18]

From this critical vantage point, it becomes clear why black men tend to see themselves as victims, even in situations where they are clearly at fault and are also in positions of power, as my father was in relationship to my aunt. Because black men who subscribe to this ideological thinking are operating within the terms of white male supremacy, their attempts to combat oppression will always already be "misguided" and doomed to fail: "The fallacy of both the strong black women–weak black men thesis attributed to gender relations of black men and women and the strong white men–weak black men thesis of hegemonic masculinity is that both counsel black men to embrace unrealistic strategies for dealing with relations of dominance."[19] Hill Collins argues that in order to move in a more constructive direction toward what she calls "progressive black masculinities," black men will have to reject "not only the images currently associated with black masculinity but also the structural power relations that cause them. In particular, uncoupling ideas about strength from ideas about dominance might enable more black men to tell the difference between the two."[20]

The question remains: How do we, as feminist-identified black men in particular, put such theories into practice, especially in black male spaces? One major obstacle in moving from theory to practice is the intense policing of patriarchy and heteronormative masculinity in black spaces. Feminist-identified men are no more insulated from the cultural sting and pressure of this policing dynamic than are feminist-identified black women against intraracial accusations of man-hating and selling out for laying claim to feminism. Black Panther Eldridge Cleaver's vicious attack on James Baldwin in *Soul On Ice* – the Ur-text of the Black Power movement – comes immediately to mind. Cleaver invokes Baldwin's sexuality and so-called masochistic attraction to white men to discredit Baldwin as a real man and, by extension, as someone qualified to speak on issues of black men and oppression. In this infamous character assassination we see Hill Collin's theory of strong white men–weak black men at play. In Cleaver's twisted patriarchal assault, he (mis)represents Baldwin as a racially self-loathing, masochistic black man who invites white rape. Meanwhile, Cleaver – who admits to raping black women as "practice" for raping white women, a move that was designed in his mind to attack white male power – imagines his brand of black nationalistic resistance as truly revolutionary.

As Mark Anthony Neal reminds us in *New Black Man,* such policing dynamics of patriarchy are alive and well today. In a rather illuminating moment in the text, Neal dramatizes how such patriarchal discourses complicate his teaching against patriarchal dominance even as he tries to press his students to rethink their homophobia and hypermasculine notions of black manhood: "I've realized that if I protest too much and openly admit to my students that I *am* heterosexual, that it makes me as homophobic as they are, because I would largely be motivated out of the fear that they would think that I *was* gay. I suspect that the various anecdotes I share with my students about my daughters are the way that I subconsciously – probably more conscious and deliberate than I want to admit – compensate for the possibility that some of my students will see me as gay."[21] Neal's confession about his fear of being labeled gay is instructive. Bound up in this label is the threat not simply of being deemed sexually deviant but rather of being stigmatized as a racial sellout, not a real man in cultural terms. Neal reveals the vulnerability that exists on this issue of black manhood for even black feminist-identified men who grasp the intellectual aspects of this gendered policing.

Personally, what I have learned from interacting with and counseling black men – from inside classrooms to inside prison cells – is that many genuinely feel powerless, socially emasculated, and worthless. These responses stem partly from their feeling under assault by what Athena D. Mutua calls "gendered racism." Mutua rightly notes that though black men benefit from unearned gender privilege in a patriarchal society, they are "nonetheless sometimes oppressed by gender and race" as a "single social position – *black men, one word.*"[22] She provides a host of statistics on black men that reveal this gendered racism, including high rates of incarceration, suicide, health care problems, and shorter life spans. Coupled with the ideas about manhood that Hill Collins outlines above, this dynamic of gendered racism means that black men are often struggling to love and respect themselves. The cultural reality that seems never to make the headlines, or even to be mentioned in private spaces, is that many black men feel insecure about their manhood and exist in a perpetual state of fear – fear of not being accepted by their male peers, fear of police brutality, fear of going to jail, fear of dying, fear of being a failure, and fear of failing the women they love and feel, however misguidedly, a strong charge to protect. The thug masculinity that has become synonymous with young black manhood in the hip hop era often covers over these fears. Indeed, the marketability of black men as thugs via hip hop culture in general and gangsta rap music in particular has meant that even black men have difficulty distinguishing between fiction and reality in their own lives. This dynamic radically swung into focus for me several years back, when I was teaching in a Knoxville, Tennessee, summer program designed to encourage underrepresented groups to attend college. One day I discussed the Oscar-nominated movie *Boyz n the Hood* to get the students to think critically about the representations of strong black manhood in the movie. To stimulate discussion I asked a young black male teenager in the front row (there were about a hundred students in the auditorium) what I thought was a rather uncontroversial question about the movie's climax. I referenced the scene in which Tre Styles (Cuba Gooding Jr.), a college-bound student, decides against riding with Doughboy (Ice Cube), a street-wise ex-con, to avenge the gang murder of his good friend and Doughboy's half-brother Ricky (Morris Chestnut), a star football player with a promising athletic career. I then asked the student if Tre made the right choice not to participate in the revenge murder. The response was a palpable silence. The young man visibly started to sweat and squirm in his seat. He then started nervously scratching the top of his head as if he had suddenly been put on trial for murder himself. Finally, after what I'm sure felt to him like an eternity – even though it was probably little more than half a minute – he pleaded: "I'm not sure, Prof. Ikard. I mean, what would you do?" In that brief and awkward moment before he finally responded to my question, I realized what a precarious position I had unwittingly placed him. Either choice held serious repercussions for how his manhood was going to be read by his peers. Choose to ride with his friends and avenge the death of his homie and he appears strong in the eyes of his peers – but will, most certainly, be challenged by his professor to defend his position and risk embarrassment. Stay at home, as Tre decides to do in the movie, and he risks appearing weak and cowardly to his friends and peers, which in this particularly case meant the other ninety-nine students – male and female – in that classroom. Luckily, I recovered in time to use my own underestimation of the tenacity of black patriarchy and notions of hypermasculinity as a teaching moment. More specifically, I engaged the students in a discussion about what made what should be a clear-cut ethical decision so daunting and complex.

Morrison captures this phenomenon of black male fear and confusion, albeit in a historical context, in Stamp Paid's response to the thinly veiled attack on his masculinity in Paul D's mock request to bunk with Judy/Judith. Stamp Paid launches into a story about his now dead wife, Vashti, who, as a slave, was coerced into having sexual relations with her married white master. Stamp Paid – whose name was then Joshua – tells Paul D that though he was furious to the point of murder over his master's actions, "I never touched [Vashti] all that time. Not once. Almost a year."[23] Though we can certainly find fault with Stamp Paid for thinking that because he didn't lash out physically at Vashti (who, fearing for his safety, convinced him not to retaliate) he has borne the emotional brunt of his white master's abuse of power, we need to register the fact that he sought an alternative to violence and blaming Vashti. Namely, he indirectly referenced the sexual exploitation to his master's wife to see if she could stop it. Stamp Paid's story is critical thematically; he opens up to Paul D in large part to prove to him that – contrary to his sycophantic behavior toward the white horseback rider – he is a real man and can empathize with Paul D's feelings of emasculation, especially as it concerns protecting black women from white rape and sexual assault. (The rub, of course, is that Paul D is displacing his feelings of impotence onto Stamp Paid. In reality, Paul D couldn't even protect himself from white rape.) We witness Stamp Paid's capacity to evolve in terms of his patriarchal thinking, when he comes to Sethe's defense later in the conversation as he tries to explain her motivations for infanticide: "She ain't crazy. She love those children. She was trying to out-hurt the hurter."[24] After Stamp Paid breaks through Paul D's emotional defenses the reader begins to see that the real source of his anxiety is feelings of social and emotional impotence and worthlessness. As for Paul D, he has virtually no social, political, or economic agency and cannot protect black women or even himself; therefore the white male hegemonic notions of masculinity that he measures his black masculinity against all but guarantee that he will fall short as a man in relation to white men. He is left with no viable discourse at his disposal to (re)negotiate his feelings and sexual abuse and to reimagine the possibilities of black manhood. Reflecting his (conditioned) self-hatred and feelings of gendered impotence, Paul D asks Stamp Paid, "How much is a *nigger* supposed to take? Tell me. How much?" Reflecting the salient limitations of his own critical discourse on the issue of black manhood, Stamp Paid responds, "All he can . . . All he can."[25]

Is it possible for Paul D to see and empathize with Sethe's consciousness and motives as a black woman if he thinks of himself as a "nigger"? That Paul D reunites with Sethe, who has experienced a nervous breakdown, at the end of *Beloved* and reminds her that "You your best thing" is certainly a cause for optimism.[26] Though Morrison does not tell us Paul D has been able to move past his feelings of self-hatred and emasculation, his encouraging words to Sethe clearly indicate that he is capable of evolving and growing insofar as his notions of manhood are concerned. The political lessons in this for feminist-identified black men are clear. If we hope to be effective in getting black men to rethink their investments in patriarchy and heteronormative manhood, ours must be a critical approach that is attentive to the challenges and obstacles preventing black men from seeing themselves, as well as the dangers, to invoke Audre Lorde, of trying to bring down the master's house using the master's tools. While there are no easy answers as to the most effective way to develop such a critical discourse and bring about these desired social and political outcomes regarding new scripts of black manhood, we can take heart from the incredible successes of the black feminist movement.

Though small in number and up against incredible odds from both within and beyond black spaces, these women managed to carve out a space in academe and the public domain to engage black women's complex humanity and era(c)ed subjectivity, even within the mainstream feminist, Black Power, and civil rights movements. What they proved was that just a handful of politically conscious activists and agitators can make a major difference. If black men want to lay claim to this incredible legacy of empowerment and resistance, we can expect no less from ourselves. The stakes are too high and costs too deep for us to do otherwise.

All I know is I want to die, but I don't want to die alone.

Paul Beatty, *The White Boy Shuffle*

Sometimes you have to laugh to keep from crying.

African American colloquialism

All Joking Aside: Black Men, Sexual Assault, and Displaced Racial Angst in Paul Beatty's *The White Boy Shuffle*

WHEN THE LAPD COPS WHO BRUTALLY BEAT RODNEY KING ARE acquitted of all charges in Paul Beatty's *The White Boy Shuffle*, we get a rare glimpse behind reluctant black leader Gunnar Kaufman's façade of racial skepticism and discursive political humor. Overwhelmed emotionally by the injustice of the verdict and the powerlessness that he feels as a black man and writer to confront it, Gunnar reports that as he watched "the [white] announcer gloat [on television], my pacifist Negro chrysalis peeled away, and a glistening anger began to test its wings."[1] When one of the African American locals suggests that Gunnar – a "street poet" – channel his feelings in a publicly displayed poem, Gunnar rejects the idea, musing that "even at its most reflective or its angriest, my poetry was little more than an opiate devoted to pacifying my cynicism."[2] Though Gunnar understands that the angry mobs that blindly attack whites are as ineffective in combating racial inequality as his poetry writing, he thinks that theirs is a more courageous and emotionally satisfying enterprise, for at the very least their violent response gives them a tangible outlet for their rage and presses the white dominant power structure to take notice and respond. Referring to poets like himself as "tattletales," "whiners," and drive-by "instigators," he concludes, "You write about blowing up the White House and they tap your phone, but only when you buy some dynamite will they tap you on the shoulder and say, 'Come with me.'"[3]

The periodic glimpses that Beatty provides into Gunnar's various states of vulnerability, confusion, frustrations, fear, and anger are crucial to understanding the political trajectory of the novel, as they give context

to what Jeanie Pyun calls the "high [racial] cost" of Gunnar's "hilarity."[4] This high cost of hilarity is reflected most dramatically in the ways
Gunnar plays fast and loose throughout the novel with the race–gender
issues about which he cares deeply and that, in many instances, have
caused him great pain. The fact that the bulk of political humor in the
novel turns on the ways in which Gunnar is perpetually misread by racial
insiders (including his family and friends) and the white male dominant elite is significant, then, beyond what it transparently reveals about
the problems of white male supremacist ideology and blacks' largely
unconscious complicity in it. Cultural misfit that he is – seeing and, in
many instances, rejecting the race–gender identities imposed upon him
from without and within black domains – Gunnar is alienated from even
those, like his best friend and basketball phenom Nicholas Scoby, with
whom he most identifies on an intellectual and emotional level. Indeed,
Gunnar's herky-jerky path toward manhood and racial self-actualization (coinciding with his movement from a nearly all-white middle-class
cultural milieu to a nearly all–black and brown working-class one, and
back again) generates as much anxiety as it does critical insight. That is,
the more Gunnar becomes aware of the ways that imposed white male
supremacist and capitalist notions of race and, more specifically, black
manhood, skew and erase his personhood, the more he becomes aware
of, and skeptical about, the limits of his agency to alter the status quo.

If Gunnar is, at times, "laughing mad" – a term Bambi Haggins uses
to characterize how blacks have historically used humor as a political
tool to cope with and express racial angst – he is, above all, "laughing
scared."[5] Meaning in this context that he uses humor as a device to negotiate and, at times, mask his feelings of fear, racial alienation, social
invisibility, and powerlessness in both black and white spaces. Indeed, a
critical issue that *White Boy Shuffle* brings to the fore via Gunnar's political consciousness and emotional vulnerability is the reality that many
black men, especially those that are poor and/or working class, exist in a
constant state of anxiety and fear. Indeed, it is an open secret among my
black male colleagues and friends that even as we are highly educated
and have acquired a level of status and financial stability, we harbor fears
of (repeat) police brutality/harassment, getting shot on the street, or
"caught up" in the judicial system. Michelle Obama illuminated this

reality in dramatic fashion when, during a *60 Minutes* interview, she was asked whether she fears for her husband's life because of the many death threats he receives as the country's first black president. She responded with candor, "I don't lose sleep over it, because as a black man . . . Barack can get shot going to the gas station."[6] When Michelle Obama says she "doesn't lose sleep over" the thought of her husband being shot because he is the first black president, she is obviously not conveying a lack of concern over her husband's safety. Rather she is pointing out that fearing for her husband's safety and the black men she loves (including her father and brother) is not a *new* racial reality, but one that she has been coping with throughout her life.

With an eye toward exposing these invisible realities of black men's emotional vulnerability and the social and cultural obstacles complicating paths beyond prescribed gender roles for black men, this chapter focuses on Beatty's "laughing scared" rendering of Gunnar's brutal rape at the hands of his father, a racially self-hating black man and LAPD police officer. I argue that the stilted and obscure ways in which Beatty introduces Gunnar's incest rape in the novel bespeak the challenges that even the author has in broaching and engaging this gendered taboo issue. We witness these challenges in Beatty's writerly "reluctance" to return to or suss out the emotional, political, and cultural implications of Gunnar's rape and, by extension, the intersecting race, gender, class, and sexuality politics that render such sexual violations against black men unspeakable. Despite this writerly reluctance, Beatty's rendering of incest rape is noteworthy, if only because he clears a pathway to consider how pervasive notions of hard/thug masculinity and heteronormativity have wreaked havoc in black men's lives. To wit, even as Beatty "skirts" direct engagement with the issue of father-son incest rape that he invokes, his novel's attentiveness to black complicity in oppression, groupthink, and the cultural need/desire for community support and affirmation shines light on exactly why such taboo and gendered discussions are difficult to broach, let alone transcend. Gunnar exemplifies this political impulse time and again via his negotiation of capitalism, hegemonic masculinity, and white male supremacy. Though he is unsparing in his attack on bankrupt racial platforms, particularly those that pit black men against each other and reinforce white male supremacist capitalism, he never loses sight of his direct and indirect participation therein. In this respect, he embodies the paradox that such a complicity-free existence cannot be fully realized but must nevertheless be strived for to develop critical insights and stave off racial despair. While he strongly encourages us to laugh at, and along with, him on his path toward political consciousness, the textual "joke" is that however absurd and pathological are the racial politics dictating race–gender realities in our society, they have, at bottom, real life and death consequences for blacks generally, and for poor black men in particular.

In his important study, *African American Satire: The Sacredly Profane Novel,* Darryl Dickson-Carr explains that the political stakes for African American satirists in the post–civil rights era are different in significant ways from their literary forebears. White oppression in the present is far less overt than in the pre–civil rights era and, concomitantly, new advances in blacks' civil rights have given rise to a more class-stratified and politically diverse black populace with, at times, diverging interests in confronting white power. Addressing the contemporary black satirists' political role in this new cultural landscape, Dickson-Carr writes,

> As a discursive descendent of the griot, the contemporary African American satirist . . . draws upon the inherent complexity of the voices that are part and parcel of black existence for material, reducing those voices to their most ludicrous level to confront them ironically. With the increasing conflict between groups on the edges of African American cultures, these voices have grown even more strident and diversified, and thus more susceptible to satiric critique. This heightened polyphony obviates an inquiry into the purpose of black satire in the post–Civil Rights era. Is it to continue to target oppressive forces within and outside the African American communities? Is it to call for a return to a less complicated past? Is it to argue for or against black cultural and political solidarity?[7]

Intensifying the political stakes for black satirists in the current moment is the precipitous erosion of civil rights gains, especially among the black poor. As many modes of black resistance, including the radical 1960s black-nationalist calls for violent revolt, have become bankable commodities of a sort and absorbed into hegemonic culture, the pressing issue confronting blacks in the twenty-first century is where to turn for "viable alternatives" for resistance and empowerment. Dickson-Carr sees Paul Beatty's *White Boy Shuffle* as particularly useful and path-breaking on this political front because it elucidates the insufficiency of civil rights strategies/mindsets in addressing present-day socioeconomic obstacles in black domains. Moreover, it accomplishes this task without collapsing into "misanthropy," positing instead that black struggle against oppression is necessary and beneficial. Dickson-Carr concludes, "ultimately, Beatty directs his satire toward a cultural scene that has mistaken style for substance, that, in the words of philosopher Cornel West, is enthralled with 'nihilism.'"[8] Dickson-Carr elaborates on how the novel reinforces West's political philosophy; he notes that Beatty's approach to combating extant forms of racial oppression pivots on what West calls a "politics of conversion," whereby people recondition themselves to embrace hopefulness over nihilism and, by extension, opt for community activism and selflessness over bouts of materialism and self-gratification that stymie racial equality.

If Beatty, as I believe, does indeed have his political sights set on attacking black patterns of nihilistic thinking and revising outmoded models of resistance, he is also concerned at a more individual and intimate level with illuminating the myriad ideological and cultural factors that make fostering this mindset, especially among young urban black men, such a daunting undertaking in the contemporary moment. Beatty illuminates this dynamic in a laughing scared episode: Gunnar discusses how his manhood is tested daily on the streets of Hillside by what he jocularly refers to as "bored Bedouins." When Gunnar encounters these Bedouins, they try to intimidate him by lifting up their T-shirts and exposing their tucked in firearms. This physical display is then followed by the verbal threat, "S'up, nigger?," to which Gunnar responds by lifting his T-shirt and flashing his weapons, which include "a paperback copy of Audre Lorde or Sterling Brown and a checkerboard set of abdominal muscles."[9] He then issues his own challenge, saying, "You niggers ain't hard – calculus is hard."[10]

As L. H. Stallings explains, to be "hard" for black men "encompasses not only the brandishing of weapons, but the acceptance of a certain physical and emotional posing and impenetrability meant to stave off the painful and suffocating oppressiveness of racism and poverty. With Gunnar's words, Beatty juxtaposes physical cool-posing with the intellectual and cultural braggadocio of one who might be considered a

punk."[11] I would add that Beatty is also drawing attention to the difficulty of creating a gendered discourse wherein black men could dialogue
with each other openly and intimately outside the suffocating ideological
boundaries of prescribed gender roles. Gunnar's characterizes Audre
Lorde's and Sterling Brown's poetry books as weapons in this instance;
as writers, they boldly engage with the interiority and complexity of black
consciousness – areas of human exploration that this hard masculine
posturing (or what Stalling, borrowing from Richard Majors and Janet
M. Billson, calls "cool-posing") necessarily forecloses. What is "hard,"
indeed, is developing a political "calculus" that will allow black men – especially in such poverty-stricken and high-stress environs – a liberating
and practical alternative to measuring their manhood against white male
hegemonic models.

Throughout his narrative, Beatty writes the possibility of this "new"
black manhood model in Gunnar's displays of masculine strength-in-
weakness. He encourages the reader to view Gunnar's various acknowl-
edgements of masculine weakness and willingness to be "punked" as the
source of his strength over his rivals and would-be exploiters. Patricia
Hill Collins explains this curious connection between gendered weakness and black masculinity: "Arrayed along a continuum, virtually all of
the representations of black masculinity pivot on questions of weakness,
whether it is a weakness associated with an inability to control violent
impulses, sexual urges, or their black female heterosexual partners or a
weakness attributed to men whose lack of education, employment patterns, and criminal records relegate them to inferior social spaces."[12] Hill
Collins further notes that these representations of black masculinity
were largely manufactured by the dominant culture as a controlling apparatus and evolved over time to accommodate the new socioeconomic
and political landscape in the United States:

> Representations of black men as beasts that were created in defense of African
> colonialism evolved into those of black men as bucks who required slavery's
> domestication, and both were followed by post-emancipation images of African
> American men as rapists and thugs who could not handle their newfound
> freedoms. These images equate black male strength with wildness and suggest
> that an allegedly natural black male strength must be tamed by family, civiliza-
> tion, and, if all else fails, the military or the National Basketball Association.
> The other end of the continuum holds representations of safely tamed Negroes,

representations such as Sambo, Uncle Tom, and Uncle Ben signify castrated, emasculated, and feminized versions of black masculinity whose feminization associates them with weakness. Once the connection is made, men can no longer be considered real men.[13]

Beatty clearly signifies on this ideological prison of black masculine weakness in the ways he delineates Gunnar's relationship with his abusive father. Largely overlooked in the literary criticism, Gunnar's twisted emotional relationship with his father, Rölf Kaufman, frames the complexity and challenges of overhauling socially prescribed notions of black masculinity. The personification of racial self-hate and white assimilation, Rölf Kaufman tries to batter and coerce Gunnar into thinking that the best strategy of black male survival is to collude with white male supremacy and to embrace nonthreatening modes of black masculinity. Further complicating this conditioning for Gunnar is that Rölf displaces the pent-up racial humiliation and angst he incurs for selling out onto Gunnar in bouts of sexual violence. Beatty divulges Gunnar's sexual abuse at the hands of his father in a stream of consciousness segment, illuminating the ways "color consciousness" (prior to his move to the "hood" and reorientation to blackness) inform his individuality and perceptions of social reality. Moving categorically in order from "Blue," "Psychedelic," "White," and, finally, to "Black," Gunnar displays the debilitating results of his social immersion into a middle-class, white, liberal ideology and, by turns, the cultural currency of his father's conditioning within this milieu. In the first three color sections, Gunnar associates the colors with redeeming childhood memories, such as playing with his white buddies on the beach or with inspiring images like "whales and dolphins frolick[ing] in the clouds."[14] When he gets to the "Black" section, however, his playful, redeeming tone collapses into gloom. The section begins, "Black was an unwanted dog abandoned in the forest who finds its way home by fording flooded rivers and hitchhiking in the beds of pickup trucks and arrives at its destination only to be taken for a car ride to the desert."[15] Gunnar's childhood memories in this section are of racial confusion and self-hate encapsulated in his shared white peer worship of a black skate pro, Tony Grimes, who was "somehow disembodied from blackness, even though he was darker than a lunar eclipse in the Congo."[16] The section culminates with images of Gunnar's racially self-hating father in a drunken rage:

> Black was a suffocating bully that tied my mind behind my back and shoved me into a walk-in closet. Black was my father on a weekend custody drunken binge, pushing me around as if I were a twelve-year-old, seventy-five-pound bell clapper clanging hard against the door, the wall, the shoe tree. Black is a repressed memory of a sandpapery hand rubbing abrasive circles into the small of my back, my face rising and falling in time with a hairy heaving chest. Black is the sound of metal hangers sliding away in fear, my shirt halfway off, hula-hooping around my neck.[17]

That Beatty chooses to present Gunnar's rape at the hands of his father in a stream of consciousness narrative is revealing in regard to the novel's perspective on black masculinity. If, as Hill Collin asserts, exhibiting weakness of any kind throws black men's claims to hegemonic masculinity into question, then acknowledging being raped by another man – even as a child – constitutes the epitome of emasculation and racial impotence. While on some level this mindset applies to white men as well (which explains why male-on-male rape and sexual molestation remain a taboo topic of discussion), the stakes for acknowledging victimization on this front are far higher for black men because of their subordinate social status. (Toni Morrison reflects this cultural reality in her complex rendering and delicate thematic treatment of Paul D and black men's rape at the hands of white men in *Beloved*.) Moreover, as the discourse of black masculinity – especially in poor, urban spaces – is inextricably tied to black authenticity and nationalism, broaching the topic of sexual assault is akin to committing cultural suicide. Beatty's stream of consciousness representation of Gunnar's incest rape can be read, then, as an acknowledgment of the real and pressing cultural stakes involved for black men in opening up and expressing vulnerability in this way.

Issues of intraracial cultural stakes aside, Gunnar's dilemma here also involves overhauling the racialized ways he has been conditioned to see himself and his socioeconomic circumstances. Indeed, what makes Gunnar's experiences of incest rape "unspeakable" in white spaces, to borrow Toni Morrison's coinage, is that he has been conditioned by his father and white society to associate blackness with moral, intellectual, and cultural inferiority. This political reality explains why Gunnar is so

captivated by Tony Grimes's seemingly transcendent racial identity –
namely, his ability to generate admiration from whites and avoid the
stigmas of black inferiority despite his phenotypically African features.
Gunnar's "cool black guy" persona is significant on this score: it constitutes, at once, the indelible mark of his father's conditioning and his
attempt to subvert that conditioning. We learn, for instance, that self-
defiling laughter is the device that Rölf employs to ingratiate himself
to whites and neutralize racial tension. Gunnar notes with tragicomic
verve, "We Kaufmans have always been the type of niggers who can take
a joke."[18] Gunnar then relays unnerving childhood episodes in which his
father forces him to laugh at the racist jokes of his father's white LAPD
colleagues. Gunnar notes that he "never laughed [at the racist jokes]
until my father slapped me hard between the shoulder blades. The heavy-
handed blow bringing my weight to my tiptoes, raising my chin from
my chest, and I'd burp out a couple of titters of self-defilement."[19] This
dynamic of jocular self-defilement spills into Rölf's job as a sketch artist,
wherein white witnesses would use his facial features as a composite for
describing black suspects: "He was thick-lipped, nose a tad bigger than
yours, with your nostril flare though."[20] Racial coward that he is, Rölf
uses these experiences as twisted teaching moments, admonishing Gunnar "that my face better not appear on any police officer's sketchpad." He
then offers his son the following skewed advice: "Remember, Gunnar,
God, country, and laughter . . . [are] the world's best medicine."[21]

Beatty reveals Gunnar's attraction/repulsion toward his father Rölf
most strikingly via Gunnar's storytelling performances about his sellout paternal Kaufman ancestry. Though Gunnar, acting in accordance
to his "cool black guy" persona, recounts the stories of his sellout male
relatives with seeming relish in the white Santa Monica classroom and
schoolyard, his conspicuous elision of his father's exploits from his ge-
nealogical storytelling reveals that the stakes of masculine representation are a lot higher and more complex than he lets on. Indeed, after
detailing the exploits of his sellout Kaufman legacy (including that of
Swen Kaufman, "the only black person ever to run away into slavery"),[22]
Gunnar confesses to the reader that he intentionally omits his father
from his "schoolyard chronicles" because "I could distance myself from
the fuckups of the previous generations, but [my father's] weakness shad-

owed my shame from sun to sun."[23] Using highly sexualized language, he expounds, "His history was my history. A reprobate ancestry that snuggled up to me and tucked me in at night. In the morning it kissed me on the back of the neck, plopped its dick in my hands, and asked me to blow reveille. Front and center, nigger."[24] Gunnar's use of rape tropes to characterize his shame toward his father's sellout exploits is telling here. As we know, the impulse to rape is driven not by sexual desire, but rather by the desire to dominate, humiliate, and control. Clearly, Gunnar's representation of Rölf as a racial buffoon and "docile and meek nonthreat" does not tell the full story. The Rölf that forces Gunnar to perform oral sex and repeatedly and violently rapes him is hardly nonthreatening. Gunnar's comical (re)presentation of his father as "docile" and "nonthreatening" can be read, then, as a coping mechanism – an attempt to reestablish control over his body and person by "clowning" his father as a self-hating racial coward.

Tellingly, Gunnar reveals his rape only to the reader, and only in an abstract rendering. Given that he associates his rape with blackness and racial inferiority, it stands to reason that he doesn't share this experience with his white Santa Monica friends. Beyond the gendered shame that is associated with male-on-male rape in an intensely heteronormative society, Gunnar has to contend with the white male supremacist discourse of black pathology that would read his rape as evidence that black men are sexual predators and morally corrupt. Though on one level the gendered racial stakes for outing himself as an incest and rape survivor are intensified when he moves to an urban working-class black space where hypermasculinity reigns supreme, Gunnar is relieved of the day-to-day pressure of fending off expectations of pathological behavior by the whites in his former social sphere. As noted in chapter 2, Athena D. Mutua coined the term "gendered racism"[25] to account for the socioeconomic disadvantages black men face as gendered, raced, and also classed beings – a phenomenon that she rightly notes is missing from conventional intersectionality of feminist engagements with black male privilege and patriarchy. Beatty signifies on this reality of gendered racism for poor urban black men both in Gunnar's violent run-ins with other black men prior to establishing "street cred" as a basketball player and street poet and in the ways the LAPD reacts to his presence in the community.

When Gunnar first encounters a brother on the street in Hillside, he tries to make eye contact "with a raised eyebrow that said, 'Hey, guy, what's up?,'" with the hope that he "would open the lines of communication." He narrates, "These silent greetings were often returned in spades, accompanied by the angry rejoinder 'Nigger, what the fuck you looking at?' and a pimp slap that echoed in my ears for a week. I'd rub my stinging cheek, dumbfounded, and find myself staring into a pair of dark sullen eyes that read, 'Verboten! Stressed-out ghetto child at work. Keep out.'"[26]

Crucial to note is Gunnar's awareness that the violence perpetrated against him by other young black men is a direct result of the stress that comes with poverty and being tagged by the police and judicial system as threatening and pathological. What to a (white) outsider may look like pathological behavior is really a sociological response to subordinate social status and a veritable police state in black communities. Beatty highlights a key source of this stress when the LAPD pays Gunnar a visit shortly after he moves into Hillside. Camouflaging the racist impulse underlying their interrogation of Gunnar, the LAPD cops explain that they are checking in on Gunnar as a means of "preventative police enforcement": "We prefer to deter habitual criminals before they cause irreparable damage to the citizenry and/or its property.[27]" With laughing scared pizzazz, Gunnar responds, "You mean you put people who haven't done anything in the back seat of your squad car and beat the shit out of 'em so you don't have to do any paperwork. Thereby preventing any probable felonious assaults on the citizentry."[28]

Gunnar's cultural immersion in this working-class black urban milieu clears the space for him to grapple more productively with his racial conditioning under his father, if not also the emotional strife of his incest rape. It is notable that during his cultural reeducation in Hillside his father is largely absent. During this extended absence, Gunnar develops bonds with black and brown men he can relate to on emotional, social, and intellectual levels – black and brown men whom, prior to his experience in Hillside, he would have viewed via the lens of his conditioned white supremacy as mindless thugs. Though Gunnar never opens up to his newly minted ghetto crew – namely Psycho Loco, the Gun Totin' Hooligans, and Scoby – about his incest rape at the hands of his father, he develops intimate bonds that, at the very least, allow him to uncouple the link between blackness and pathological behavior. We see Gunnar's emotional maturity in his first moves to vocalize his anger toward his father. When his sisters lament the fact that their father has shunned them because they have moved to the 'hood, Gunnar responds, "Fuck that nigger."[29] He repeats the statement later in the narrative via an email to his sisters when they become pregnant and contemplate moving back in with their father because of a falling-out with their mother. Though he remains reluctant to flesh out the emotional and mental harm that has been done to him as a result of his father's incest rape, a key difference in Gunnar's second iteration is that he makes the source of his anger more clear and warns his sisters – albeit indirectly – to be on guard against their father, especially if it turns out that they give birth to boys: "I'm sorry to hear you all and Ma aren't getting along because of the pregnancy thing, but I can't believe you'd rather live with Dad than stay at the hippo house. You know my motto: Fuck that nigger. If you have boys, make sure you don't leave them alone with him."[30] This moment is as close as Gunnar comes in the novel to addressing the emotional anguish and suffering of his incest rape. Regrettably, the reader never learns what, if anything, comes of the letter. Do his sisters heed his word? Does Gunnar's mother learn of the abuse and confront the father? Does Gunnar ever discuss the matter openly with his mother and/or sisters?

Judging from his mother's siding with his father over sending Gunnar back to a white environment for schooling after Gunnar's involvement in stealing a safe from Montgomery Ward, it seems highly unlikely that Gunnar has broached the subject with his mother. As I discussed in chapter 2, black women's loyalty to black men can be intense, overwhelming even self-preservation and the impulse to protect children. Given this cultural reality, there is certainly no guarantee that Gunnar's mother and/or sisters would have stood against Rölf even if they were aware of his sexually abusive behavior.

What is clear is that Beatty resists romanticizing Gunnar's and progressive black men's abuse and empowerment. Beatty accomplishes this task by putting Gunnar's unique incest rape crisis in political conversation with the emotional and social struggles facing black women, the black poor, and even abusive men like Rölf. The brutal (sexual) beatdown that Gunnar receives at the hands of his father in Hillside as a result of his looting activities during the L.A. riots offers useful insights into Beatty's political impulse. Beatty sets up the encounter by having Gunnar distract his father and the other LAPD officer while Psycho Loco and Scoby drive off with the stolen safe from Montgomery Ward. Gripping a phallic "shotgun in one hand," Rölf begins to batter Gunnar mercilessly about the mouth and body. The thematic significance of this scene warrants quoting it in its entirety:

> When I turned to face my father, the hard rubber butt of the shotgun crashed into my jaw. I saw a *flash of white* and dropped to the pavement. My father's partner stepped on my ear, muffling his words.
>
> "You are not a Kaufman. I refuse to let you embarrass me. You can't embarrass me with poetry and your niggerish ways. And where did you get all these damn air fresheners?"
>
> Something hard smacked the side of my neck, sending my tongue rolling out of my mouth like a party favor. I could taste the salty ash on the pavement. Ash that had drifted from fires set in anger around the city. I remembered learning in the third grade that snakes "see" and "hear" with their sensitive tongues. I imagined my tongue almost bitten through, hearing the polyrhythms of my father's nightstick on my body. Through my tongue I saw my father transform into a master Senegalese drummer beating a surrender code on a hollow log on the banks of the muddy Gambia River. *A flash of white* – the night of my conception, my father twisting Mama's arm behind her back and ordering her to "assume the position." *A flash of white* – my father potty-training me by slapping me across the face and sticking my hand in my mushy excrement. Soon my body stopped bucking with every blow. There was only *white* – memories, no visions, only the sound of voices.[31]

In this scene Beatty repeats the phrase "flash of white" three times, both as a way to describe Gunnar's blows and to segue into childhood flashbacks of his father's physical and sexual brutality against Gunnar and his mother. The invocation of whiteness recalls the earlier stream of consciousness scene in which Gunnar thinks through his identity via a color spectrum. As discussed earlier, this stream of consciousness scene exposes Gunnar's racial self-loathing conditioned at the hands of his father – racial self-loathing that prompts him to associate his incest rape with blackness and, specifically, black inferiority. It is significant, then, that here the color white is associated not with uplifting and redeeming qualities, as was the case in the stream of consciousness scene, but with sexual violence and emotional crisis. In the first "flash of white" blow/ moment Gunnar recalls what appears to be either a planted memory or something that he has deduced from interacting with his parents – that he was conceived as a result of rape and violence. This is a crucial revelation in that it puts Gunnar and black men's gendered racism in direct conversation with his mother and black women's experiences of suffering, including at the hands of domineering and abusive black men. Under scrutiny is the long-held idea that black men's violence toward black women is a direct result of white oppression and thus should not be held against black men. What Beatty suggests in this scene is that even as white oppression does not trump individual agency – that is, black men cannot simply displace the blame of abusing black women squarely on the shoulders of abusive white men – it does play a central role in corrupting the lines of communication and intimacy between the sexes. In Rölf's particular case, brutalization under white oppression has warped him to the point of siding with the oppressors rather than the oppressed. He doesn't get a pass on his behavior, however, because even as he has been scarred by white oppression (consider the vicious racist hazing by his white peers as a teenager and then later in the LAPD as an adult), he ultimately possesses the agency to decide how he is going to respond to it. As the second "flash of white" blow/moment dramatically reveals, Rölf chooses to displace his feelings of emasculation and racial inferiority on to those even weaker than himself, including his son and wife.

It is also noteworthy politically that Gunnar's metaphoric incest rape occurs in the midst of the L.A. riots. An LAPD police officer and willful enforcer of white male supremacy and capitalism, Rölf is clearly on the wrong side of the racial conflict. Though Gunnar ostensibly rejects violence as the path to racial empowerment, as witnessed by his tag-team mock beating of the white Wonder Bread truck driver with Scoby, he fully comprehends and, indeed, empathizes with the cultural impulse to riot and loot. In the scene cited above, Beatty registers this political reality through the plunge of Gunnar's tongue onto the pavement so that he tastes the "ash that had drifted from fires set in anger around the city."[32] This connection also reflects Gunnar's lack of a viable outlet, like the rioters, to channel his anger and pain as an incest rape victim.

Beatty's attempt to insert humor into this scene (notice the line about air fresheners) exemplifies the "laughing scared" impulse of the novel. Clearly, incest rape, domestic violence, and police brutality are no laughing matters. Though it is certainly debatable whether Beatty's comedy "works" here, as the violent/pornographic nature of the scene provokes outrage and sadness instead of laughter, the narrative gesture to move past silence on such taboo raced and gendered issues is useful and redemptive.

Indeed, what is empowering about this signifying gesture as it pertains to Gunnar's incest rape is that it wrests emotional control from the grip of such race/gender shaming discourses. Chris Rock's raucous routine about male-on-male incest rape in "Bigger and Blacker" comes immediately to mind in this context. In his routine Rock jokes about a "molesting Uncle Johnny"; everybody in the family knows about him, but they cope with the situation not by calling the police, but by being hypervigilant when children are in Uncle Johnny's presence. In a revelatory moment that bespeaks how incest violence is turned back on the victimized, Rock quips, "Later on you get molested and your momma gets mad at you." Taking on the voice of the accusing mother, he fires, "That's what you get! Hanging around fuckin' Johnny. I told you about that shit. Now walk it off."[33] By voicing the unspeakable in this instance – that incest rape of black boys occurs in black spaces and is often covered up by family members, including mothers – Rock at once confirms the reality of such painful events for black men and boys and parodies the pattern of the cover-up. The comic-tragic joke, of course, is that one cannot simply "walk off" incest rape as if it were a scratched knee suffered during a sporting event or on a playground. Recovering from such an experience is more than a notion, especially considering the aforementioned stigmas against black men's weakness coupled with the gendered patterns of cover-up that typically protect male victimizers. The cultural risks for breaking the silence in such instances are so high for victimized black men and boys that they rarely reveal their sexual assaults to their family or the public at large. By satirizing such heteronormative behavior in ways that highlight the absurdity of allowing a known sexual predator within one's family to have unsupervised access to young boys, Rock manages to turn the tables on the shaming cultural discourse that silences victims of sexual assault and allows sexual predators to hide in plain sight.

Beatty's most salient attempt to upset this shaming discourse in the novel is his rendering of Rölf as a racial coward and buffoon. Beatty shows, for instance, that Rölf displaces his racial cowardice and feelings of inferiority onto his son (and wife) because he is too much of a weakling to stand up to his white peers. To this degree, Rölf emerges as a chump: someone to be pitied and even despised, but certainly not feared. This explains why, despite being beaten to a pulp by his LAPD father, Gunnar emerges from this scenario looking heroic. It occurs to me, however, that Beatty seems reluctant to push the issue of incest rape into the foreground of the novel. After the beating scene, Beatty abruptly shifts back into a satirical mode. As Gunnar blacks out from the beating he hears a cacophony of voices from friends and family, all of which – with the lone exception of his mother – make light of his situation. Coach Shimimoto mockingly calls him a "young revolutionary" and then quips "while you were in a coma, you got ... chosen as one of the hundred best ballplayers in the nation. Actually, you're number one hundred." Scoby says, "Dude, you got fucked up," and Psycho Loco adds, "You gots to get better, cuz. We can't figure out how to open the safe."[34]

Echoing his curious rendering of Gunnar's rape at the hands of his father earlier in the novel, Beatty avoids direct engagement with and articulation of this symbolic incest rape. This phenomenon becomes clear in the ways that Gunnar's friends and family respond to the beating alternately as an act of parental intervention and one of police brutality, but not rape or even child abuse. Even Gunnar's mother – who, the reader learns, has also been raped by Rölf – seems oblivious to the abuse. As stated earlier, she sides with her ex-husband abuser, agreeing to bus Gunnar to a rich, overwhelmingly white high school for cultural reprogramming.

This pattern of indirect engagement about incest rape is certainly curious in a novel that is so raw and unapologetic in its interrogation of race, gender, sexuality, and class taboos within and beyond black spaces. From a writerly critical perspective, Beatty's heightened sensitivity to fleshing out this issue bespeaks the challenges of airing such a taboo subject in the public domain generally and in black heteronormative spaces in particular. Indeed, Gunnar's infatuation with death (which has received the most critical attention within literary scholarship) can be read as a symptom of his incest rape – a cry for help, if you will. In "Black Crisis Shuffle: Fiction, Race, and Simulation," Roland Murray usefully engages Beatty's strategic framing of death and suicide in the novel, particularly in regard to black notions of empowerment from slavery to the present day. Murray astutely argues that Beatty's aim on this score is to illustrate the cultural ways that blacks have employed death and particularly suicide during slavery (as Gunnar alludes to in the poem "Give Me Liberty or Give Me Crib Death") as a means of self-determination and/or rebellion against white oppressive forces. Murray asserts:

> In Beatty's work death provides no utopian opposition against late capitalism. Even as Beatty evokes the legacy of death in slavery, he insists that the fantasy of black agency must also be subject to the primacy of the problematic that attends contemporary political economy. This approach contains an implicit charge that insisting on the utopian possibility of the slave's death is in some sense to evade the quandaries of contemporary political economy.[35]

Murray rightly identifies the ways that Beatty's satirical treatment of death-as-liberation usefully calls attention to blacks' inextricable ties to political economies – past and present – that commodify blackness for social, cultural, and economic gain. Murray points to Gunnar's sado-masochist act of cutting off his finger to make his case, arguing that the move is politically bankrupt, not only because Gunnar is insincere, but because he gets the idea from a 1974 neo-noir gangster movie *The Yakuza*, starring white actor Robert Mitchum.

While Murray's critique of death in *The White Boy Shuffle* is illuminating insofar as blacks' conscious and unconscious complicity in contemporary political economy is concerned, he overlooks the crucial relationship between this death trope and Gunnar's thinly veiled anxieties about his incest rape. It is crucial, for instance, that Gunnar's death infatuation precedes the speech about death at the anti-racist college rally that catapults him to black messiah status. In fact, Gunnar discusses a fear of dying in an email to Scoby while he is at the Nike basketball camp. Beatty introduces this section in the novel – which consists of a series of emails that Gunnar writes to his friends and family while at basketball camp – soon after Gunnar's symbolic incest rape at the hands of his father during the L.A. riots. The email addressed to Scoby that appears immediately after Gunnar's aforementioned warning to his pregnant

sisters about their father is particularly instructive. Gunnar reveals that
he is having intense nightmares about death. On one such occasion, he
wakes up screaming, sweating, and shaking. He is so loud, in fact, that
he wakes up and frightens his two roommates, Z-Groove and Touch.
Gunnar explains, "I didn't know what the hell I was carrying on about.
All I knew was that it [the nightmare] had to do with death. Like I was
running through different scenarios of how I'd like to die."[36] Though
Gunnar desires to have a substantive conversation about his nightmare
with his roommates, they cannot move past their hypermasculine poses
to engage Gunnar on a deeper emotional level. That Z-Groove is openly
queer is telling politically, for, on the one hand, it highlights the tenacity
of hegemonic black manhood and, on the other hand, it deromanticizes
the received idea that queer identity is necessarily progressive.[37] Con-
sistent with their internalization of hypermasculine identity, the best
that either Z-Groove or Touch can muster when pressed to talk about
dying is a conversation that glorifies death in decidedly heteronormative
and cavalier ways, like getting gunned down after dunking a basketball.
Disrupting their banter, Gunnar confesses, "All I know is I want to die,
but I don't want to die alone."[38] As Gunnar's failed attempt at suicide
demonstrates later in the novel, his true desire is not to die, but rather
to move past the isolation of feeling like a freak and outcast for being
raped by his father.

The White Boy Shuffle is at bottom a novel that pokes fun at the coping mechanisms of racial allegiance, hypermasculinity, and racial violence that appear on their face to be empowering, but actually do more
to hamper true transformative politics. While Beatty should certainly
be applauded for broaching such a taboo subject as incest rape for black
boys, one wonders how much more effective the move might have been
had he foregrounded the issue and employed the same take-no-prisoners
approach that informs the rest of his political engagements in the novel.
But then again, art is not so easily reducible to political formulas. As Toni
Morrison reminds us, the "test" of a writer's power is her ability to "familiarize the strange and mystify the familiar."[39] Beatty's accomplishes this
goal in The White Boy Shuffle, if only because he interrogates pervasive
notions of black manhood and offers us a black male incest rape survivor
protagonist who inclines readers to laugh at and with him rather than

to pity him or view him as a freak. To this end, it is instructive that the novel closes with Gunnar lovingly bathing his baby daughter Naomi as he tells her about the demise of her abusive grandfather who commits suicide by "eating his gun."[40] Even though at first glance it may seem that Beatty leaves the reader holding the bag insofar as knowing how to apply Gunnar's insights in transformative social ways, he gives us our answer – or, at the very least, points us toward it – precisely in this playful and tender father-daughter moment. Gunnar's tenderness – "I dip Naomi in the Jacuzzi and rub baby oil into the creases of her arms"[41] – is a far cry from the violence on display when Rölf forces toddler Gunnar to put his hand in his own shit during potty training. Despite his childish antics and discursive engagement with black agency, Gunnar emerges as a hero in the novel (not to be confused with a dubious black messiah figure) because he manages to endure his brutal social conditioning under his self-hating and abusive father without falling into the racial trap of self-hate or repeating the cycle of abuse. Breaking such a wicked cycle of abuse is nothing if not transformative.

It is certain, in any case, that ignorance, allied with power,
is the most ferocious enemy justice can have.

James Baldwin

Nothing in the world is more dangerous than
sincere ignorance and conscientious stupidity.

Martin Luther King Jr.

FOUR

Boys to Men: Getting Personal about Black Manhood, Sexuality, and Empowerment

A FEW YEARS AGO MY TEN-YEAR-OLD SON ELIJAH CAME HOME from school singing the lyrics to Soulja Boy's hip hop anthem "Pretty Boy Swag" and rehearsing the dance move that the song gave birth to. While I was more than a little amused watching my bookish and rhythmically challenged son rehearse his swag trot, my fun was brought to a screeching halt when he began to recite the lyrics. Even though he was singing the so-called PG version of the song, the R-rated messages of misogyny and playa-masculinity were coming through loud and clear. As I value Socratic modes of parenting, I decided to engage my son in a discussion about this pretty boy swag phenomenon in ways that I hoped would resonate with him. I started the discussion by asking Elijah to define the term "pretty boy." He responded that a pretty boy was kind of like a pimp; someone that looked attractive and that all the girls really liked. Rather than explain to him what a pimp really was, I made him look the word up in the dictionary and read the definition aloud. As he was reading the definition to me, his mouth gaped open in disbelief. "You still want to be a pimp?" I asked rhetorically when he was finished reading. "No," he responded earnestly. "Why would anybody want to be a pimp? That's messed up." Given that I teach my son to embrace anti-sexist modes of masculinity, he immediately grasped why referring to himself as a pimp and celebrating playa-masculinity was problematic. If I was comforted by my son's response once he understood the meaning of the words that he was singing, I was stunned at just how insidious and pervasive these destructive notions of black masculinity have become in the twenty-first century.

After my talk with my son I decided to investigate the lyrics to the song further to see what else he was being exposed to. I discovered that the song was also virulently homophobic. At one point in the song Soulja Boy spits, "I'm pretty boy swaggin' in the club I feel sexy / No homo shawty but my chest is straight flexin."[1] The expression "no homo" in hip hop culture is shorthand for "I'm not a homosexual." This expression is used almost exclusively by black men and typically in circumstances where men are expressing affection toward one another or articulating themselves in a way that could be deemed weak or unmanly. Given that the label "pretty boy" denotes a black man who places a high premium on his overall appearance and uses charm and charisma rather than brawn and thuggery to seduce women, someone who self-identifies as such would be particularly vulnerable to being maligned by his male peers as a "homo" or a punkass. When Soulja Boy says that he "feels sexy" in the club – a statement that tends to be associated with women not men – he follows with the line, "No homo shawty but my chest is straight flexin,"[2] in a clear signal to heteronormative black men that he is indeed straight despite his suspect language use.

It's important to note that this "no homo" phenomenon is not indigenous to hip hop culture, the whipping boy of a host of conservative institutions, including many so-called respectable black institutions such as the black church. Baptist minister and popular CNN pundit Roland Martin is a case in point. He made headline news when he tweeted several blatantly homophobic remarks during the 2012 Super Bowl. The most egregious involved comments about a titillating commercial that featured sculpted soccer superstar David Beckham in seductive poses modeling his new line of men's underwear. Martin tweeted that men who liked the commercial were not "real bruhs" and that people should "smack the ish" out of them.[3] When Martin first encountered pushback from gay activist groups and individuals over his tweets, he shrugged it off, claiming that he was joking and that his words were being taken out of context. Though Martin's tone changed from dismissive to apologetic after the controversy became headline news and CNN temporarily suspended him as a pundit, he never owned up to his homophobia. Indeed, since his rather brief suspension from CNN he remains widely popular and has even emerged in black church culture as a martyr.

Moving back closer to home, I recall a telling incident of homophobia and black masculine posturing that occurred several years ago when
I was at a college football game with my father, who is a highly respected
deacon in his church, and my younger brother, who is a Bible school
teacher and youth director. During halftime, all of us headed to the restroom before the start of the third quarter, laughing, joking, and signifying on each other as only black men can do. When we walked into
the restroom our chatter suddenly stopped. To our surprise, the stalls
were not individually partitioned. There was just a trough-like urinal
that ran the length of the restroom wall. Everybody was exposed, so to
speak, as they used the restroom. The awkward silence that fell over us
when we walked into the restroom wasn't broken until after we left. My
younger brother did the honors. He said that he thought he saw someone
checking him out while he was using the restroom and was prepared to
punch the imagined offender in the jaw. My father chimed in that he
was thinking along the same lines, that he too suspected that he was
being watched. I should add that we were the only black men in the
restroom and a conspicuous minority in the stands – which is to say we
were under intense surveillance from the moment we stepped into the
arena. Our unexpected exposure in the restroom simply illuminated our
surveillance as black men and potentially threatening sexual beings in
a white male–dominated space. As I listened to my father and brother
work themselves up into a head of steam over this phantom white gay
man checking them out, I was struck not only by the violence and venom
of their homophobic bantering, but also by what they seemed unable or
unwilling to express – namely, that being exposed like that among all
those white men made them feel insecure and threatened. This male
bonding ritual between my father and brother – which required invent-
ing a gay Peeping Tom to verbally beat to a pulp – provided a way for
them to address these unspeakable feelings of insecurity and fear. In a
word, this was their version of the "no homo" qualifier.

While it should go without saying that black men are no more or less
homophobic than white men (consider the fact that Barack Obama is not
only the first black president but also the first to openly endorse gay marriage), their racial subjectivity as men radically alters the stakes of their
masculine negotiations. Indeed, the fact that R&B rising star and hip

hop songwriter phenom Frank Ocean's and NBA player Jason Collins's coming out was headline news is a rather salient case in point. Given that society continues to treat heterosexual white middle-class manhood as normative and black manhood, by comparison, as deviant and pathological, the blind pursuit of normalcy and respectability for black men in the (white) public domain renders them complicit in the very discourses of power – including heternormativity – that sustain the status quo. But this complicity is complicated to identify and root out: even though black manhood, like all gender identities, is socially constructed, it nevertheless informs and, in some instances, dictates how black men, particularly those with limited education and resources, are treated in almost every facet of society. Kobena Mercer offers useful insights into this phenomenon, explaining that black male gender identities have been constructed historically and culturally through complex dialectics of power and subordination.[4] He argues that stock images of black masculinity, ranging from Uncle Tom to hypermasculine figures like Shaft (and I would add the gangsta drug dealer), have been "forged in and through the histories of slavery, colonialism and imperialism."[5] Invoking Robert Staples's insights on the relationship between contemporary iterations of black manhood and slavery, Mercer explains that a central tenet of white men's historical assertion of racial power over black men was to deny them access to the spoils of hegemonic white manhood, including the ability to own property, have familial responsibilities, and the like:

> Through such collective, historical experiences black men have adapted certain patriarchal values, such as physical strength, sexual prowess, and being in control as a means of survival against the repressive and violent system of subordination to which they were subjected. The incorporation of a code of "macho" behavior is thus intelligible as a means of recuperating some degree of power over conditions of powerlessness and dependency in relation to the white master subject.[6]

To underscore his point about white male hegemony and black manhood, Mercer gives the example of how young black men in Britain end up reproducing and maintaining gendered racial stigmas of black thuggery despite themselves. Even though, historically, black men have had to be tough in order to stave off sanctioned state and police violence against them, the reality of this self-defensive posture has been erased from the public discourse, making it appear that black men are inherently and pathologically angry and violent, constituting a threat to white citizens that must be contained at all cost.

While Mercer does not purport to know how to resolve these issues for black men, he rightly argues that black men need to begin to take their political cues from black feminism and black queer theory in order to see how patriarchy – which fuels sexism and homophobia – is the enemy of black men's empowerment. Intersectionality – the idea upon which black feminist theory is premised – holds that all oppressions are interlocking and must be confronted as such in order to upset status quo power relations. Building on this idea, black queer theory makes the case that heteronormativity means that raced, gendered, and classed experiences of black queer communities remain largely invisible or unacknowledged in black empowerment politics. Indeed, from Malcolm X's claim that black lesbianism was a symptom of failed black manhood to Eldridge Cleaver's attempt to discredit James Baldwin as a black spokesman on the basis of his homosexuality and so-called sadomasochist desire to be raped by white men and father their children, queer identity has historically been read in black spaces as pathological, emasculating, and counterrevoluntionary.

Homophobic comments like those Roland Martin posted to Twitter are constitutive of this longstanding cultural mindset. The rub is that this thinking also reinforces the hypermasculine notions of black identity that continues to have major social, cultural, and economic repercussions for black men. Consider the tragic case of Trayvon Martin, a black teenager who was "mistaken" as a thug-criminal in his own neighborhood by a white Hispanic neighborhood watch captain, George Zimmerman, and then stalked and killed. Based on the 911 calls that Zimmerman made to the Sanford, Florida, police department, it is clear that the extant idea of black boys and men as inherently criminal governed how he read and reacted to Trayvon's presence in "his" community. The official narrative that emerged from the case and that the Sanford police department helped to orchestrate is that somehow Zimmerman, who stalked and killed Trayvon, was the true victim. Not only did the Sanford police department test Trayvon to see if he had drugs in his system and neglect to do the same to his killer, but they also failed to investigate Trayvon's cell phone registry, which would have revealed that he was actually on the phone with his girlfriend trying to figure out what to do about the strange white man who was stalking him. Moreover, part of the reason that it took so long to arrest Zimmerman was that under the stand your ground law in Florida – which was made into law under Jeb Bush's administration at the behest of the N R A (National Rifle Association) – the use of lethal force is allowable even if one of the individuals in a dispute is armed and the other is unarmed. Thus, Zimmerman's claim of self-defense under the stand your ground law, coupled with the pervasive idea of organic black male criminality, provided more than enough to exonerate him – initially that is – in the eyes of the police force and district attorney's office.

Tellingly, Roland Martin was one of the leading voices in the Zimmerman arrest debate, decrying the racial profiling of black men that prompted the white neighborhood captain to target the innocent black teen. The reality is that Martin indirectly contributed to this dynamic of profiling in his hypermasculine and homophobic tweets. Though he addresses the problems and consequences of Martin's homophobic "joking," Charles Blow's insights on Martin – whom he claims as a friend – apply equally to these tropes of black hypermasculinity and thug-criminality. Separating out Martin's intent from the consequences of his words, Blow explains that even if Martin was joking (and Blow believes he was), the problem is that

> in the real world – where bullying and violence against gays and lesbians, or even those assumed to be so, is all too real – "jokes" like his hold no humor. There are too many bruised ribs and black eyes and buried bodies for the targets of this violence to just lighten up and laugh. We all have to understand that effects can operate independent of intent, that subconscious biases can move counter to conscious egalitarianism, and that malice need not be present within the individual to fuel the maliciousness of the society at large.[7]

If the unintended effect of Roland Martin's words is that they fuel homophobia and gay-bashing, they also fuel the notion that real black men are hard and aggressive. This is precisely the kind of portrait of black manhood that whites – past and present – have used to justify everything from vigilante lynching in the post–Reconstruction era as a necessary safeguard against a "scourge" of black rapists of white women to the now infamous stand your ground law in Florida, which allowed

Zimmerman to claim self-defense and avoid arrest for nearly fifty days despite clearly being the aggressor and deploying lethal force. Indeed, we see this racial calculus at work in the operating assumption for the police and the media that the stand your ground law applied to Zimmerman and not Martin. This is a crucial oversight, as the law states that a citizen has a right to stand her ground in a space she has the legal right to occupy and that there she may legally defend herself, even with lethal force, if she feels "threatened." It took black journalist Charles Blow to expose this operating racial assumption and introduce the idea that the law applied equally to Martin, who was killed in his own neighborhood while presumably defending himself and standing *his* ground.

My point here, to return the problems of Roland Martin's statements, is not simply that Martin and patriarchal black men are unwittingly complicit in the stereotyping of black men, but also that their investments in heteronormativity – which is inherently raced and classed – frustrates more expansive and complex notions of black men's humanity. Given that white stigmas of black men as prone to violence, gangsterism, and drug abuse (which happens to be substantially higher among whites in general)[8] continue to influence how the dominant culture sees black men's humanity, black men can ill afford to cosign (with silence) and/or actively perpetuate the widely embraced version of black hypermasculinity that Roland Martin parroted in his tweets and public rhetoric. It is important to keep in mind too how class, social status, and education inform the treatment of certain black boys and men in white spaces. Roland Martin is *not* Trayvon Martin. Aside from sharing the same last name, these black men have very little in common when it comes to social and class status, education, and celebrity. There's little debating, for instance, that Roland Martin can thrive in spaces like CNN precisely because of these advantages and his attendant mastery of hegemonic white expectations of (nonthreatening) black manhood. Tim Wise calls this raced phenomenon "enlightened exceptionalism." Unlike previous generations of whites who made little, if any, classed distinctions among blacks, whites in the twenty-first century routinely extend "honorary whiteness" to a select group of blacks (think Barack Obama, Oprah Winfrey, Sidney Poitier, Halle Berry, Will Smith, and Roland Martin) that they deem exceptions to the rule of black inferiority. As Wise observes, enlightened exceptionalism "manages to accommodate individual people of color, even as it continues to look down upon the larger mass of black and brown America with suspicion, fear, and contempt."[9] These whites feel "enlightened" because they experience this more sophisticated brand of racism as progressive racial thinking.

What enlightened exceptionalism means for black men in particular is that those bestowed with honorary whiteness like Roland Martin are not soft targets for white oppression, even though they are not completely shielded from racism. Henry Louis (Skip) Gates's ability to fight and win against the Cambridge police department after being arrested for what Michael Eric Dyson aptly called "housing while black" is but one glaring case in point. The reality is that most black men (including those who benefit from enlightened exceptionalism) embrace some version of gangsta/playa/pimp/hustler masculinities because doing so is a necessary coping and/or survival mechanism. Moreover, some see these masculine performances as oppositional, empowering, and "authentic," even though in actuality they neither disrupt nor challenge structural inequalities and white male dominance. Though race, gender, and sexuality are social inventions designed in large part to control and police bodies and, by extension, to make the value system of the dominant group (in this case, elite white men) synonymous with normalcy, the real and material consequences of being raced, gendered, classed, and sexualized mean that most black men experience these invented categories as social realities rather than social fictions. This sociological phenomenon is precisely why many black male scholar-activists who identify with black feminist and queer politics are often on the outside looking in when it comes to debating such matters within our own cultural communities. Rather than give us credibility, our progressive gender and sexuality politics, coupled with our advanced degrees and learning, often mark us as whitewashed, elitist, out-of-touch, and untrustworthy at best, and soft, traitorous, unmanly, and Uncle Tom–ish at worst. The academy's long and sordid history of discrimination, unethical experimentation on black bodies, and racist propaganda masquerading as scholarship exacerbates matters even further. Who but a severely compromised black

man would think that black feminism and queer studies have something
to teach black boys and men about self-determination, black resistance,
manhood, eroticism, and intimacy?

Mark Anthony Neal cuts to the quick of this dilemma for feminist
and queer-identified black scholar activists when he opens up about the
risks involved (real and imagined) for challenging revered notions of
what he calls "Strong Black Manhood." According to Neal, Strong Black
Manhood grows out of the widely respected legacy of race men, span-
ning the decades, from Prince Hall, Martin Delaney, W. E. B. Du Bois,
Booker T. Washington, and Alexander Crummell to, more recently,
Louis Farrakhan, Maulana Karenga, and Al Sharpton. These men embody cultural values that are noteworthy and redeeming, including having a deep love of and commitment to black folks, a willingness to defend
black femininity "in a chivalric nature like that historically afforded to
white women," and providing financial support to their families as well
as "stability, honor, and discipline for . . . [their] children, particularly
in a society that has historically deemed black men as lazy, shiftless,
indifferent, and parasitic."[10] The problem is that many of these revered
Strong Black Men (think also Roland Martin) have "been unrepentant
in their sexism, misogyny, and homophobia."[11] The cultural capital of
Strong Black Manhood is so intense that the men who endorse such
biases are rarely held accountable. Neal explains the tenacity of this
cultural practice:

> When our mythical black nation is under siege and in crisis, the only thing
> that is not allowable, especially when at war, is the demise of the "Strong Black
> Man." And according to some pundits . . . the black man is *always* at war – at
> war with "the white man," at war with "the system," and at war with *his woman*,
> the black woman. To some, to acknowledge some of these shortcomings or to
> scrutinize these men and hold "some damn body" accountable, is to attack the
> "Strong Black Man" and thus attack the very foundation of the black nation.
> Even worse, it's an attempt to collude with our enemies to bring down the
> race.[12]

To challenge Strong Black Manhood as a straight man is to undermine
one's cultural claim to traditional masculinity and the spoils of cultural
acceptance that are inextricably tied to it. Neal articulates this gendered
cultural tension when he poses the following question to himself and

other like-minded black men: "How willing am I to undermine my status within traditional black masculinity by claiming the politics that most 'Strong Black Men' would consider the politics of a 'punkass'?"[13]

In his iconic text *Why I Hate Abercrombie and Fitch: Essays on Race and Sexuality,* Dwight McBride explains the political stakes involved for queer black men for taking similar risks in challenging revered notions of black manhood and cultural respectability. McBride is particularly concerned about the risks as a gay black man of discussing "the gay marketplace of desire."[14] He openly displays his anxieties of bearing witness to his experiences, including the fear that he will be shunned as a traitor by other black gay men who "made this most private of journeys and maintained a code of silence about it."[15] He also fears that he will be misunderstood by "outsiders" and do more harm than good in his attempt to elucidate gay black men's complex humanity. Concomitantly, his biggest fear is that anti-gay opponents will use his experiences as "proof of the 'depravity' of gay male sexuality."[16] Rather than allow these fears to silence him, McBride takes his political cue from black lesbian feminist trailblazer Audre Lorde and shares his experiences "even at the risk of having [them] bruised and misunderstood."[17] To the degree to which he wants to clear a space for gay black experiences beyond the social realm of respectability (where black gay icons like Lorraine Hansberry, James Baldwin, Bayard Rustin, Josephine Baker, and others reside), McBride's stance resembles that of gay black poet and literary giant Langston Hughes. Though he was addressing the issue of respectability and blackness, Langston Hughes's aforementioned essay, "The Negro Artist and the Racial Mountain," aggressively challenged status quo notions of black humanity, pointing out – among other things – that the double-consciousness thinking propelling (elite) blacks to sanitize the funkiness of their lived experience in white eyes is itself dehumanizing. Even as Hughes never explicitly broaches homosexuality, his argument about *un*sanitizing blackness for the sake of white acceptability clears a space for seeing "deviant" sexualities and eroticisms as constitutive of blacks' complex humanity and not markers of racial shame or pathology. As McBride makes clear in his argument, the political hurdle – then and now – in challenging intraracial taboos and airing dirty laundry is that doing so will inevitably come at great costs. Chief among these costs for McBride and black gay men is risking cultural isolation even within black queer communities. This social reality explains in part why black queer academic testimonials of the kind that McBride engages in his book are few and far between. One-man armies tend not to be all that difficult to defeat.

As an antihomophobic and black feminist–identified black man, my most pressing challenge is helping my son develop the critical models and emotional resilience to resist the unrelenting pressure to accommodate the gendered/raced status quo that Neal and McBride outline above. Developing such a parental model is difficult in large measure because so much of it relies on creativity and invention. As parents, most of us rely – consciously and unconsciously – on the models of parenting that our parents employed to guide our way. While there are certainly redeeming aspects of my rearing that I can and do recycle as a parent, much of it – particularly as it concerns my son and manhood – runs counter to my progressive masculine politics. As I mention in chapter 2, I grew up in a Southern conservative Christian household that, while progressive in some ways when it came to women's role (my mom has a lot of feminist sensibilities), was very much steeped in patriarchal and heteronormative culture. Indeed, my father epitomizes the Strong Black Man cast – a status, I might add, that allowed him to be criminally abusive toward girls and women with social and cultural impunity. Of course, when I was a child these abusive behaviors were difficult to discern, because, as Neal points out in *New Black Man,* black communities give Strong Black Men like my father plenty of political cover. From my vantage point as a child and boy, my father appeared to be nothing short of heroic. He was a man's man, as the saying goes, and I wanted to be just like him. While the issue of sexuality in my small Southern environ was never openly discussed in private or public settings (save an occasional sermon about the evils of homosexuality), it loomed large in my cultural consciousness, because – unspeakable though it was – it defined my very personhood as a boy. To this day, I've never heard my father utter the word "homosexual," "queer," "faggot," or "gay," including the episode at the football game I outlined earlier. As I think back, the first time the issue of homosexuality was ever broached openly between my father and me was during my sophomore year at North Carolina State

University. I was starring in George Wolfe's *The Colored Museum,* and my parents made the three-hour trek to Raleigh from our small town to see me perform. It was not my performance (I played the soldier in the "Soldier with a Secret" sketch and the kid in the "Symbiosis" sketch) that sparked the discussion, however. It was a superb student-actor and gay black man (we'll call him Damien) that played the fiery snap queen/race man Miss Roj in "The Gospel According to Miss Roj" sketch. No stranger to violent gay-bashing or cross-dressing, Damien played the role of Miss Roj to chilling perfection. His performance brought down the house. When I discussed the play with my father over dinner that night, he wanted to know how Damien was able to move so well in high heels. When I responded jocularly that Damien had plenty of practice because he was a cross-dressing gay man, my father was unnerved. He responded incredulously, "You mean he's" – and, instead of uttering the word "gay," "homosexual," or "queer," he held up his right hand and shifted it back and forth horizontally, his generation's sign language for queer. And that's where the conversation ended. It was these types of unspeakable and unspoken messages that informed and policed my sexuality as a boy and man. Homosexuality – which was culturally synonymous with un-manliness – was the othered masculinity against which our performance of acceptable masculinities was measured.

Though my father – like many Strong Black Men of his generation – was certainly guilty of policing heteronormativity, some of this polic-ing was informed by the life-and-death realities of racial survival. As working-class black boys and men in the deep South in the 1970s, our bodies were constantly under surveillance. Practically from birth, we were taught as boys to be hyperaware of the threat our bodies posed to whites generally and white men in particular. For instance, one of my father's rules for his sons was that we had to wear a shirt outdoors at all times, regardless of the heat index. The only exception to this rule was when we went swimming at the lake or YMCA pool. As a child I remember thinking that this was the silliest rule in the world. The white boys in my neighborhood and at school hardly ever wore shirts during the scorching summer months. I never understood the logic behind this rule – which my father enforced with a vengeance – until I was an adult and became more conscious of the threat that black male bodies posed to white male dominance.

The other thing that was off-limits when I was a boy, of course, was dating white girls. It was an open secret in my small Southern town that whites would not tolerate interracial dating (that is, black men dating white women; the reverse – which was rare – did not elicit the same response). In 1990 – the year I graduated from high school – a black star football player and neighbor was ambushed and severely beaten at his doorstep when the word got out that he was dating a white cheerleader on the DL. I also recall several black boys being kicked off the football team for such infractions, even though this reality was obscured in the official narratives. I had more than a few conversations about the subject with white boys when I was in high school, and they would openly admit that a white girl who dated a black boy was essentially "ruined" as a marriage prospect in their eyes. White manhood – then and now – was premised in large part on "protecting" and controlling white women's bodies (think Thomas F. Dixon Jr.'s novel *The Clansman: An Historical Romance of the Ku Klux Klan,* and D. W. Griffith's blockbuster movie *Birth of a Nation* based on it). Within the gendered script of white patriarchy, white women symbolized white virtue and moral purity. A self-respecting white woman within this script would readily choose death over losing her chastity to a black man. My white male peers' resistance to interracial dating derived in part from this white male supremacist logic. Though obviously by the 1980s white men could no longer deny the fact that some white women welcomed and pursued the sexual attention of black men, many sought to punish such white women with stigmas and cultural ostracism. Even though black men were constructed in white male narratives of power as sexually infatuated with white women, the truth was that black men's attraction to white women was generated, in part at least, by white men who tethered access to white women's bodies to social prestige and masculine power. To gain access to white women's bodies was to gain access to the policed domains of white male power. Even though laws prohibiting interracial marriage, along with white terrorism, lynching campaigns, and the like, were effective in keeping the number of interracial relationships low, these restraints also eroticized interracial sex in ways that are still evident today, especially in the porn industry. It is hardly a coincidence, then, that black male writers from Richard Wright, Ralph Ellison, Chester Himes, and Eldridge Cleaver to, more recently, Edward P. Jones, Paul Beatty, and Percival Everett have engaged this discourse in some form. Indeed, the most worried I have ever seen my father was when I decided as a junior in high school to invite an attractive white girl (we'll call her Julie) with whom I was close friends to accompany me to a county-wide basketball tournament. No doubt afraid for my safety, my father sat me down that same night and relayed a story about a black man in our community who was murdered for allegedly dating a white woman in the early 1980s. Though I didn't scare easily – particularly when it came to fighting racism – the fear in my father's eyes as he was relaying the story shook me to the core. Though I continued to hang out with Julie, I was certainly much more cautious of where we went.

The complexity of black men's humanity and the diversity of our individual experiences means that we each respond to this raced and gendered climate of surveillance in a range of ways, even if the pressure to conform weighs heavily on us all. I felt this pressure most acutely during my junior and senior years in high school, when I was often the only African American in my college prep courses. Many of my working-class black peers racially politicized my course track, some going so far as to label me a wannabe or sellout. Even though the absurdity of these claims was not lost on me at the time (I couldn't control who enrolled in college prep courses), they were still quite hurtful in tangible ways. (I recall an African American girl at the time who openly admitted that she was reluctant to date me because of this stigma.) The racist social climate in my small town meant that black students received little, if any, encouragement to pursue college unless they happened to be a standout athlete. Most, in fact, were steered away from college prep courses and encouraged instead to enlist in shop courses or join the ROTC with an eye toward military service. I was enrolled in college prep courses, then, not because I was so much smarter than my black peers, but because I bucked the system and refused to let myself be ghettoized academically. Paul Beatty underscores this racist paternalism in *The White Boy Shuffle* when, on the first day of classes at his new elite white San Fernando

Valley high school, protagonist Gunnar Kaufman checks in with the guidance counselor, who treats him like a charity case and intellectual flunky. After the counselor gives Gunnar a week's worth of lunch money and tries to steer him into remedial courses despite his high IQ and test scores, Gunnar responds sardonically, "I appreciate your eleemosynary concern, but have you checked my [academic] records?" The stunned counselor returns, "My elemen . . . elmo . . . my what?" Gunnar then follows, "Just stop patronizing me and do your job. Treat me as an individual, not like some stray cat that you feed once a day."[18]

This climate of systemically suppressing black academic achievement was the modus operandi at my high school. Unfortunately, it gave rise to an oppositional identity that conflated high academic achievement with acting white. I should clarify that this acting-white calculus is not static across black spaces. The unique racial politics of my school was the driving force behind how the black students responded to academic achievement. It wasn't that they didn't want to do better; rather they were led to believe that race and class limited their options for social advancement. Their environment reinforced this view, and thus many caved to white expectations of black mediocrity. Accordingly, my refusal to do so was misread as a desire to be white.

Further exacerbating my circumstances was the growing popularity at the time of gangsta rap, which gave rise to thug masculinity and black gangsta culture. Indeed, thug-masculinity – defined by street credibility, criminality, resistance to the (white) police force, and prison culture – quickly became synonymous with authentic black manhood. I witnessed young black men in my community – including my best friend and cousins – transform right before my eyes from starry-eyed choirboys to wannabe, and in some cases real-life, drug dealers and gangbangers. One of my cousins – who had sustained several gunshots wounds while hustling on the block – was sentenced to twenty-five years in the state penitentiary for drug trafficking and possession of illegal firearms. My best friend was incarcerated for similar offenses. Another drug-dealing cousin just barely escaped a prison sentence because the arresting officer turned out to be a dirty cop who was shaking down drug dealers for cash. Three more kids in my neighborhood were killed in gang-related activities. Though I was never down with the thug life posture (which is not

to say that I didn't get down with gangsta rap at the time), I did derive a
level of gendered cultural currency from my status as a varsity athlete. (I
played football, basketball, and ran track. I was also on the swim team,
but because it is considered a white sport, it detracted more than added
to my gendered cultural capital among my black peers.) Looking back, I
suspect that my status as an athlete was my saving grace where proving
my manhood and racial "realness" were concerned, because it neutralized much of the criticism I incurred from taking the white college prep
courses.

Because the discourses of power that do us the most damage emotionally, culturally, politically, and physically also happen to be the most
difficult to pin down and name, I – like far too many black men in America – was walking around with a rather large (racial) chip on my shoulder
throughout most of my young adult life. However destructive were the
hypermasculine black modes of masculinity, they offered black men
and me a (false) sense of self-determination and empowerment. On my
roughest days in college when I was feeling particularly fed up with the
racial micro- and macroaggressions that come with being a black man
on a majority white Southern college campus, I would go to my dorm
room and blast gangsta rap music. N WA's "Fuck the Police" single was on
regular rotation as was Ice Cube's "AmeriKKKa's Most Wanted" album.
As much as I needed an avenue to vent my feelings of anger, frustration,
fear, anxiety, and pain, I also needed a way to organize and understand
them, to think beyond the imposed gendered expectations of black and
white communities. My exposure to African American literature and
theory in college and then black feminist theory during graduate school
were a godsend to my self-actualization, providing the critical frameworks to help me to see and productively grapple with my race, class,
and gendered subjectivity as a black man in America. Black feminism
was particularly useful in this regard; it helped me to see the ways in
which prescribed racial expectation of hypermasculinity – from within
and beyond black spaces – were hurting black women and undermining
black empowerment across racial lines.

But, alas, my journey to political consciousness has been rocky at
best. And, of course, I am still on that journey and am reminded daily,
by my lapses into unproductive patriarchal behavior and thinking, that

I am not yet where I'd like to be on this political front. If my son has advantages that I didn't have, they are that he has a father – indeed, an extended network of folks, including his mother and aunt, who are black feminist academics – from which to draw guidance, support, and insights on what it means to be an empowered anti-sexist, anti-homophobic, and pro-black African American man. Even though my son has these advantages, I suspect that his journey toward empowerment will have its own unique obstacles. As the Trayvon Martin case has brought radically into view, stereotypes about black men as violent and threatening abound, despite the fact that we have reached a point in our collective history when a black man can be elected to the highest office in the land. More egregious than even this racial reality is the fact that we have been conditioned as black men to be afraid of each other. Black men are killing each other at a far greater rate than anyone else. What's more, there seems to be little political will in the White House or other seats of power to address the extant socioeconomic factors that have generated this phenomenon. We see this reality borne out in the proliferation of zero tolerance laws and policies (from the classroom to the city streets), which disproportionally impact people of color.

As grim as the future looks for black boys and men in America (sky-rocketing incarceration rates, dismal unemployment, alarming high school dropout rates, and largely stalled upward mobility), I find comfort in the political strides that have been made thus far by progressive-thinking black folks in pressing black men to think more critically about our gendered subjectivity as black men, especially as it relates to empowering black women and interrogating imposed and destructive modes of sexuality and black manhood. If, as the popular African American colloquialism goes, "hurt people hurt people," it is also the case that empowered people empower people. I am reminded of the truth of this latter statement when I witness my son sticking up for bullied kids and taking his (usually male) peers to task for their homophobic, sexist, and racist comments and jokes. Which is not to say that my son never falls into the patterns of patriarchy and heteronormativity from time to time, but rather that he possesses a productive critical model to think about his subjectivity as a raced, gendered, classed, and sexualized being (as the anecdote that opens this chapter brings to light). Indeed, he rightly takes me to task from time to time for failing to practice what I preach on this score. If I occasionally lose sleep at night worrying about how my starry-eyed, precocious son will fare in a world where it is still possible for black boys to be gunned down with impunity, I take heart in the fact that my budding scholar-activist is not afraid *to stand his ground* against racism, homophobia, classism, and sexism. A father couldn't be more proud of his son.

I destroyed white baby dolls.
But the dismembering of dolls was not the true horror. The truly
horrifying thing was the transference of the same impulses to little
white girls. The indifference with which I could have axed them
was shaken only by my desire to do so. To discover what eluded me:
the secret of the magic they weaved on others. What made [even
black] people look at them and say, "Awwwww," but not for me?

Claudia in Toni Morrison's *The Bluest Eye*

Good hair means curls and waves /
Bad hair means you look like a slave

"I Am Not My Hair," India Arie

FIVE

Rejecting Goldilocks: The Crisis of Normative White Beauty for Black Girls

IT CERTAINLY STARTED OUT INNOCENTLY ENOUGH. MY CHILDREN'S elementary school was having a book parade to generate enthusiasm about reading. Each child was encouraged to come to school dressed as their favorite character in a book. My then nine-year-old son, Elijah, who had just recently finished a book report on Muhammad Ali, decided he wanted to dress as the iconic boxer and civil rights leader. My outspoken, feminist-minded, six-year-old daughter, Octavia, wanted to be Goldilocks from the classic story *Goldilocks and the Three Bears*. Given the intense messages about normative white beauty that pervade our society and that I have personally witnessed shaking my daughter's confidence in her African beauty and personhood, I was deeply troubled by my daughter's choice. Indeed, prior to this moment I'd noticed a preoccupation on my daughter's part with skin tone and hair texture. "You and Elijah are dark-skinned but mom and me are lighter," she said one day out of the blue when we were at the park. "We're all African Americans, baby girl," I had responded and left the matter alone, hoping against hope, as the saying goes, that she had not already begun to internalize the colorist/white supremacist politics that still permeate our society. When shortly thereafter she made a comment about wishing she had hair like a white girl in her class, I realized there was more to the issue than I had first registered. This book parade issue, in fact, materialized right as Octavia's mother and I were preparing to sit down with Octavia and discuss these issues of colorism, black beauty, and self-esteem. (We'd had a similar discussion with my son when he was around the same age.) Suffice it to say, her choice to dress as Goldilocks set off many red flags for me and I felt compelled, given her recent comments, to intervene. Instead of vetoing Octavia's choice outright, I tried to engage her about the racial significance of her choice, to use this opportunity as a teaching moment. I asked, "Why do you want to be a blond-haired blue-eyed white girl? You have tons of books about smart and beautiful girls of color – why not choose to be one of them?" (We do not own *Goldilocks and the Three Bears,* by the way. I learned later that Octavia had borrowed a copy from the school library.)

Perhaps worn out from a long day of activity (it was getting close to her bedtime) and rightly sensing that she was being set up for another one of her daddy's countless "teaching moments," Octavia opted not to engage my probing question. She didn't even ask why Elijah had gotten his first choice of characters and hers had been questioned. Knowing my daughter as I do, I could tell that she was not happy with my challenge against her choice. Rather than voice her discontent, though, she consciously rejected my not-so-subtle suggestion that she choose a character from one of her many books about girls of color. The book she chose instead was one that she had only expressed a lukewarm response to, about a baby fox who gives her mother grief because she wants to stay up all night to play instead of sleep. "Can I be a fox, then, daddy?" she asked rhetorically, trying to assert her provisional agency. "Why do you want to be a fox, now?" I pressed, more than a little annoyed that she was not cooperating with my teaching moment ploy. "So, I can't be a fox, either?" she whined with a smirk on her face. Aware that things were going awry and I had been *outfoxed* by a six-year-old, I let the matter go, making a mental note to myself that I needed to contact Octavia's mother and expedite our plans to talk with her about the aforementioned racial politics. My immediate concern at the time, though, was getting to the store that night to purchase props for the book parade the following day. Where on earth was I going to find a fox outfit for Octavia at the eleventh hour?

The next morning, when I presented my children with their costume props for the parade – boxing gloves for Elijah and a fox mask and tail for Octavia – they were very excited. Octavia, in particular, seemed particularly delighted with her costume, which gave me the *false* impression that the Goldilocks issue was not as pressing a matter as I had first assumed. My misreading of the situation became apparent shortly after dropping them off at school. At about 10:00 A M that morning, I received a cryptic message from Octavia's young Southern white teacher Mrs. Johnson (not her real name), which read: "I just wanted to give you a heads up, for the future, that anything you say (good or bad) always comes back to school. I tell my parents that I generally only believe ½ of what my students tell me about them as long as you believe only ½ of what you hear about me. I think that Elijah has a working filter, but Octavia just shares what she hears. Just food for thought."

As I have a good rapport with Mrs. Johnson, I was confused and a bit alarmed by the coded language. So, instead of just responding to the email, I called the school and asked to speak with her directly. Turns out, that Octavia was very upset and quite vocal about my steering her away from her first choice to dress as Goldilocks. According to Mrs. Johnson and Elijah (who was evidently walking beside Octavia in the parade), Octavia blurted out that her daddy wouldn't let her dress as Goldilocks for the parade because he didn't want her to be a white girl. As best I can surmise, Elijah intervened to explain to Mrs. Johnson that Octavia was taking my words out of context (which explains Mrs. Johnson's comment about Elijah's "filter"). Clearly disturbed by Octavia's comment, if ultimately not knowing how to think about them given her experiences with me, Mrs. Johnson sent me the cryptic email.

Coincidentally, this drama unfolded in the midst of black history month and during a series of lessons that Mrs. Johnson was teaching on racial tolerance. Though her motives were certainly good, Mrs. Johnson's approach to teaching race was decidedly postracial. That is to say, she discussed racism as passé and emphasized – à la Martin Luther King's iconic "I Have a Dream" speech – that people should be judged on the content of their character not on the color of their skin. As I have stated elsewhere, African Americans – most especially the poor and working class – cannot afford to confuse the ideal of postracialism with the *reality* of extant racial and structural inequalities.[1] It should go without saying that the stakes for such confusion are quite different for whites, many of whom benefit socially, economically, and mentally from era(c)ing this reality. Indeed, a recent study in the field of psychology by Michael L. Norton and Samuel R. Sommers reveals that many whites now believe that anti-white bias is more prevalent in the United States than anti-black bias. The authors write, "This emerging perspective is particularly notable because by nearly any metric – from employment to police treatment, loan rates to education – statistics continue to indicate drastically poorer outcomes for Black than White Americans."[2]

Such blindness is particularly harmful to black girls and women, whose unique marginalization as gendered beings in black spaces and the public at large continues to be trivialized by the dominant culture as self-inflicted, misappropriated by other oppressed groups for political advantage,[3] or just outright dismissed. To be clear, when I say gendered beings here I am not ignoring the reality that black men are gendered beings as well; rather I am speaking to how the variable of gender informs the experience of blackness and personhood for black girls and women. To wit, black girls and women's unique and intersecting race, gender, and class subjectivities mean that they must not only contend with the debilitating and patriarchal images of ideal femininity that negatively affect *all* women, but also with a white (male) hegemonic discourse that tethers ideal beauty and femininity to whiteness. My impulse to steer my daughter toward a culturally affirming image of black girlhood was an offensive move, meant to expose and disrupt the messages about whiteness and beauty that pervade our society and that had inevitably impacted my daughter's self-perception *despite* her parents' heightened political vigilance. The pervasiveness of these notions was dramatically borne out in Mrs. Johnson's response to me when I acknowledged that I had indeed steered my daughter away from dressing as Goldilocks. She (mis)read my proactive, anti-racist gesture as racist. With a tone of righteous indignation, she lectured, "I think insisting that Octavia dress as a girl of color is kinda racist. Shouldn't she be free to choose her own character regardless of race? I mean, what can be more harmless than Goldilocks?" Mrs. Johnson's response is typical of postracial thinking. Postracial logic holds that the "new" racists are not those who have what Eduardo Bonilla-Silva calls the "embodied racial power" of white skin,[4] but those (typically oppressed people of color) who see race and racism as still having a major social and economic impact on blacks and people of color in general.

Morphing into instructor mode, I tried to explain to Mrs. Johnson that the postracialist message she was sending my daughter and her students was premised on lofty ideals rather than material racial realities. Far from having transcended race, we live in a society in which institutionalized racism continues to inform and, at times, dictate social and economic outcomes for African Americans. During my conversation with Mrs. Johnson – who was politely dismissive of my perspective as only Southern white women can be – I kept thinking how absurd this all was. Here I was – a target of racism and countless microaggressions all my life – pressed into defending my fatherly gesture toward my daughter to someone with white privilege and the faintest clue about blacks' lived experience. And here's the rub. I genuinely believe that Mrs. Johnson has my daughter's best interest at heart. But, as James Baldwin writes in *The Fire Next Time,* "It is the innocence which constitutes the crime."[5]

In this chapter I want to engage the challenges that black girls face in the United States, including the aforementioned postracial politics and white hegemonic notions of femininity and beauty, and think critically about how blacks generally and black men in particular can play a positive role in empowering black girls. While the urgency in black spaces to focus on black men's issues, including skyrocketing incarceration rates, police brutality, intraracial violence, delinquent fatherhood, and the like is understandable, given the dire socioeconomic circumstances of black men and boys in this country, such urgency often comes at the expense of ignoring the plight of black women and specifically black girls. The patriarchal thinking that still reigns supreme in black spaces is that the fates of black girls and women hinge on black men's success, or lack thereof, in acquiring traditional (read: white) masculine status, power, and agency. Thus black girl and women's issues are always already subordinated to the concerns of "masculinating" and empowering black men. Premised on normative (white) gender roles, wherein the male is the primary breadwinner and the woman the primary caregiver-nurturer, this male-centric cultural thinking in black spaces contributes to pervasive (white) ideas about black women as overly strong, manly, angry, and unmanageable. (Michelle Obama is the latest and most visible example of the tenacity of this stigma. Despite her professional demeanor and even-tempered disposition, she has been attacked as an "angry black woman" by whites on the political left and right, before and since becoming First Lady of the United States.[6])

The undergirding and rarely uttered thinking in black spaces is that black women need to take their political, social, and cultural cues from middle-class white women, at least insofar as they pertain to yielding authority and breadwinner status to their male counterparts. It is historical fact that black women's breadwinner status came about because black men's exploited labor and disenfranchisement at the hands of white men in the post-slavery era forced black women into the workforce as a means of economic survival; nevertheless, black women's breadwinner status is often viewed as an attack on black manhood, especially if said women do not adhere to what Patricia Hill Collins calls "hegemonic femininity" and yield to the patriarchal authority of the men in the home. Because of this pervasive mindset, black women have become the go-to scapegoat in and beyond white spaces to explain a range of black social problems that stem largely from extant institutional racism and structural inequalities. The 1965 Moynihan Report, which tagged black women as pathological and held them chiefly responsible for the socioeconomic failure of black men, is but one of many examples of this phenomenon.

What all of this means is that the unique challenges and obstacles that black women and girls face are often invisible, obscured, or devalued in the very cultural spaces that they most depend on for support and affirmation. Given these cultural realities, it is not difficult to see why my daughter and black girls would gravitate toward (white) normative images of white womanhood and beauty. They are inundated socially with messages, overt and subliminal, that signal to them that black girlhood is somehow lacking or less available than white girlhood. Take for instance the intraracial notion of "good hair" that originated from white supremacist ideology and remains alive and well in black spaces today. The notion holds that blacks have "good hair" if it is finer textured hair, like that of whites, as compared to the thicker and coarser Afrocentric hair. To have "good hair" as black women – particularly if one was also endowed with lighter skin and Eurocentric facial features – was to be in possession of a physical attribute that in black spaces was as good as gold. The idea is so pervasive in black communities that it spawned a comedy documentary by comedian Chris Rock. Rock says that he was prompted to create the documentary by his five-year-old daughter, Lola, who asked him one day, "Daddy, how come I don't have good hair?" In the documentary, we learn that the business in black hair is a booming nine-billion-dollar enterprise. Though Rock inserts a lot of humor into the documentary, the glaring reality that shines through time and again is the extent to which white standards of beauty – especially in terms of hair texture – continue to dominate black consciousness.

I should preface my remarks here by noting that white male supremacist notions of beauty radically inform white women's notions of beauty as well, and inevitably impact their self-esteem – as evidenced by the link between eating disorders among white women and received notions of ideal beauty – and also the billions of dollars a year they spend on beauty products, including wigs, weaves, hair extensions, and plastic surgery. Indeed, as one of my black feminist scholar colleagues reminded me, white beauticians invented and ushered in the trend of wearing wigs, weaves, and extensions. That said, what becomes clear in Rock's documentary as it concerns black women, beauty, and self-esteem is that conditioned black inferiority is a bankable commodity. The rub is that most of the capital generated from the black hair industry does not benefit black communities. Because it is taboo in many black spaces to discuss the relationship between this black hair phenomenon and hegemonic (white) femininity, interventions of the kind that Rock launches in his comedy documentary are extremely rare and almost always uncomfortable. The cultural challenges of engaging in substantive and critical debate about the racial politics of black hair was humorously on display in the interviews that Rock conducted in the documentary. Discussions that involved the widespread and expensive practice of putting in hair weave were particularly instructive. Though the relationship between white standards of beauty and black women's intense investment in weaves is undeniable in the documentary (some interviewees openly admitted forgoing necessities and even paying rent to maintain the hairdo), few of the black interviewees experienced this relationship as a serious problem. In a rather stunning moment in the documentary, Rock interviews four black female high school students about the politics of hair, asking them specifically about what they think would be an acceptable hairdo for African American women in corporate America. All of them, with the exception of a lighter-skinned woman sporting a natural hairdo, say that they will either straighten their hair or install weave when they seek

employment after graduation, because they don't think that they can
land jobs otherwise. By far the most hilarious and illuminating scene in
the documentary occurs when Rock tries to sell parcels of African hair
weave to several beauty stores in Los Angeles that specialize in black
hair care products. All the stores refuse to purchase the hair, noting that
blacks weren't interested in buying it.

I should make clear here that the relationship to these hair-styling
techniques and white supremacist ideology is not cut and dried. In *Welcome to the Jungle: New Positions in Black Cultural Studies,* Kobena Mercer cautions us against oversimplifying this racial calculus and reading
processed hair (he doesn't discuss hair weaves) as a symptom of racial
inferiority. While he acknowledges that "black people's hair has been
historically *devalued* [by white Europeans] as the most visible stigma
of blackness, second only to skin," and that the move to process hair
is bound up in this ideological reality, he explains that the other factors – like the creative elements of black hairstyling – reveals that blacks
are not just acquiescing to dominant white power.[7]

> From a perspective informed by theoretical work on subcultures, the question of
> style can be seen as a medium of expressing the aspirations of black people his-
> torically excluded from access to official social institutions of representation and
> legitimation in urban, industrialized societies of the capitalist First World. Here,
> black people of the African diaspora have developed distinct, if not unique,
> patterns of style across a range of cultural practices from music, speech, dance,
> dress and even cookery, which are politically intelligible as creative responses to
> the experience of oppression and dispossession. Black hairstyling may thus be
> evaluated as a popular art form articulating a variety of aesthetic "solutions" to a
> range of "problems" created by ideologies of race and racism.[8]

To Mercer's point, altering black hair texture and styling to conform
to more Eurocentric models cannot be read myopically as a reflection
of distorted racial consciousness. Longtime political activist Al Sharpton – who has sported a processed hairdo for several decades – is a striking case in point. In *Good Hair* he explains that his choice to relax his
hair was influenced by singer and black power icon James Brown. Inci-
dentally, Brown introduced the idea because he wanted Sharpton, who
was accompanying him to the White House to meet Ronald Reagan and
agitate for a Martin Luther King holiday, to look like him as a form of
kinship and political solidarity.

That said, the reality is that this "depsychologized" notion of black hair and beauty, to borrow Mercer's language, is already the dominant perspective in black spaces. As Rock's documentary accurately conveys, most African Americans in the twenty-first century do not psychologize the link between black hair styling and white male supremacist ideology. Thus the problem is that the white male supremacist politics that still radically dictates what counts as "good hair" and good looks has been normalized. Indeed, most black folks experience their hair and cosmetic choices as a matter of taste rather than ideology.

Melissa Harris-Perry's special segment about black hair on her television show – which constituted one of the rare occasions in which black women were given a platform to speak critically about issues of black hair – offers additional insights into the relationship to between black hair, racial politics, cultural creativity, and self-esteem. Though Harris-Perry opens this segment with a lighthearted commentary about black hair that seeks to educate and depoliticize black hair for her white viewers, who are apparently obsessed with her braids, the bulk of the show, which featured black feminist journalist Joan Morgan, actress Nicole Ari Parker, University of Pennsylvania professor Anthea Butler, and CurryNikki.com founder Nikki Walton, made clear that black women's hair choices/styles remain as politically and racially charged as ever. Later in the show Harris-Perry confirms the reality of how whites politicize black hair and vilify black women: she invokes the controversial 2008 cover of the *New Yorker* featuring a cartooned depiction of Barack Obama, in an Arab headdress and robe, giving a fist bump to his wife, Michelle. The First Lady, rendered with an automatic assault rifle slung across her back, sports an afro – not typically her hairstyle of choice. Though the illustrator of the cover, Barry Blitt, intended the portrait as a satire on right-wing conspiracy theories, it actually provided even more ammunition for the radical right. Harris-Perry is skeptical about the received political intent. She opines that the afro smacks of a political scare tactic, the idea being to make Michelle appear "radical." Shifting the discussion to intraracial matters, Joan Morgan questions what it means that folks are now robbing black hair salons for their expensive assortment of hair weaves – hair that in many cases was acquired via illegal or coercive means in the first place – and unloading them at a premium price on the street. She goes on to describe black women's investment in hair as an "addiction" and "another kind of pain that we're not comfortable addressing." Hinting at the psychological toll that hair politics wreaks on black women's consciousness, Nicole Ari Parker recalls fellow actress Tracie Thom's insightful comment about natural black hair in Rock's documentary: "It's amazing that it's considered revolutionary to wear my hair as it grows out of my head."[9]

Even as the panelists deftly probed the tension between hairstyles and cultural politics, the issue of extant white supremacy and how it continues to inform and complicate black hairstyle choices and notions of black beauty in general was conspicuously glossed over. While a natural hair movement is afoot – popularly known as "transitioning" – and African loc extensions are trending (Chris Rock probably didn't see that coming), our cultural notions of what constitutes beauty have not been radically altered over the last century, nor has our conditioned negativity toward dark skin and Afrocentric features. My suspicion is that these issues constitute the "pain" Morgan was referencing that black communities and black women in particular are not comfortable addressing. The problem, of course, is that the elephant in room – extant white supremacy – remained unnamed throughout the segment. This made it all the more curious that Harris-Perry chose to end the show with a feel-good moment where she introduces and prompts us to praise a white man who adopts an African girl and learns to do black hair. If the move was designed to make her white viewers feel hopeful and included, it also cast light on the problematic capital of white empathy (is a white man doing black hair really deserving of such praise?) and the political efficacy of white surveillance (this discussion did take place, after all, in the studio of a major network).

WHITEWASHED BLACK BEAUTY

Historically speaking, the market demand for whitewashed black beauty is inextricably tied to slavery, where colorism – which is merely an extension of white male supremacist ideology – was aggressively cultivated by white middle-class slave-owners. Though slavery was debilitating for all African captives and their descendants, lighter-skinned blacks – most often the result of exploitive sexual relationships between white masters and enslaved African women – were elevated by whites within the pecking order among the enslaved. For instance, the enslaved lighter-skinned Africans were often picked to work in the master's house and thus avoided the heat and the toll of working in the fields. Working in the house also came with the advantage of eating better, as house slaves typically ate the master family's leftovers, which were substantially better than the food that was given to the field slaves.

Living in the house and in closer proximity to whites came with its own risks, however, as house slaves – including men and boys – were often the targets of white sexual assaults. Moreover, slave women raped by or coerced into sex with their masters usually had to contend with the wrath of the white mistresses, who blamed enslaved women, rather than their white husbands, for the relationships and the children that typically resulted from them. Moreover, laws were put in place that shielded white men from culpability in raping and impregnating black women. Escaped slave and abolitionist Frederick Douglass – the product of such a relationship – expounds on this legalized system of rape and sexual exploitation in *The Narrative of the Life of Frederick Douglass:* "Slaveholders have ordained, and by law established, that the children of slave women shall in all cases follow the condition of their mothers; and this is done … to administer to their own lusts, and make a gratification of their wicked desires profitable as well as pleasurable; for by this cunning arrangement, the slaveholder, in cases not a few, sustains to his slaves the double relation of master and father." Crucial to note here is a key distinction in how escaped slaves like Douglass and Harriet Jacobs in *Incidents in the Life of a Slave Girl* discussed such sexual exploitation and how it was (re)presented in white abolitionist literature, in the form of the archetype of the tragic mulatto – a mixed-raced character, usually a woman light enough to pass as white. She is "tragic" because, even though she looks white, her "black blood" taints her in some way, preventing her from fitting into white society and even alienating her from the "lowly" blacks. The white abolitionist literature that played on the tragic mulatto archetype rarely, if ever, challenged whiteness as normative and, by extension, the idea that white beauty is superior. Indeed, it was the whiteness of these black women characters that rendered them worthy of white empathy.

So even (white) interventions ostensibly designed to attack slavery in the nineteenth century were premised on raced notions of beauty and normalcy and driven by a white paternalistic impulse.

White paternalism aside, black women have been especially impacted by these notions of white beauty over time. The reality is simply this: most black women do not fit this white beauty ideal. Consequently, many darker-skinned women have felt inadequate and even ashamed of their dark skin and African features. As Ayana D. Byrd and Lori L. Tharps note in *Hair Story: Untangling the Roots of Black Hair in America,* "Although both [black] men and women were evaluated by this standard [of white beauty] it was traditionally women who internalized it, as women are most commonly evaluated on looks first and all other criteria second."[10] Patricia Hill Collins echoes these insights in *Black Sexual Politics:*

> Because femininity is so focused on women's bodies, the value placed on various attributes of female bodies means that evaluations of femininity are fairly clear cut. Within standards of feminine beauty that correlated closely with race and age women are pretty or they are not. Historically, in the American context, young women with milky White skin, long blond hair, and slim figures were deemed to be the most beautiful and therefore the most feminine women. Within this interpretative context, skin color, body type, hair texture, and facial features become important dimensions of femininity. This reliance on these standards of beauty automatically render the majority of African American women at best as less beautiful, and at worst, ugly. Moreover, these standards of female beauty have no meaning without the visible presence of Black women and others who fail to measure up. Under these feminine norms, African American women can never be as beautiful as White women because they never become White.[11]

The reality of this gendered cultural phenomenon was brought radically into focus during a 2011 summer program in which I taught high school and middle school teachers about African American and black popular culture. A young, attractive, darker-skinned female elementary school teacher recalled how as a teenager she frequently received "compliments" about her appearance from black men such as, "you're really pretty for a black girl." As dark skin and African features are still largely understood as socially undesirable, most especially for black women, the boys and men who say such things to darker-skinned black girls and women genuinely experience their degrading colorist comments as compliments. Given the pervasiveness of such conditioned biases against darker-skinned women, I suspect that more than a few darker-skinned black girls and women tolerate the slight in silence.

During this summer program another dark-skinned teacher, who taught high school and was a cheerleading coach, shared a disheartening experience that she had with a darker-skinned female honor student of hers. When discussing the issues of marriage and relationships with said teacher one day, the student disclosed that she planned to marry a white man so that she could have beautiful fair-skinned babies. Deeply disturbed by the operating racial assumptions that informed her student's thinking, the teacher used the situation as a teaching moment. She asked the student why she felt that lighter-skinned babies were necessarily more attractive than darker-skinned ones. "What do you see when you look in the mirror; when you look at me?" the teacher asked rhetorically. "Has it ever occurred to you that you are beautiful just as you are; that you should be proud of your appearance? That if your children were born looking like you then they'd be beautiful as well?" According to the teacher, the student had never considered such possibilities, had, in fact, been articulating her desires to have light-skinned babies among her friends and family for years without any pushback. Based on the racial messages that she was receiving from the media and even within familial spaces, her self-deprecating colorist thinking seemed completely rational.

From hip hop videos and movies to fashion magazines and even video games, the message that darker-skinned women are the most unattractive women on the planet is hard to ignore. Complicating matters, colorism has long been a taboo subject in black spaces, and consequently there is not a productive discourse in place to suss out its impacts on black consciousness and particularly that of black girls and women. This is a serious problem, considering that stigmas associated with dark skin and African features remain rampant in and beyond black spaces. Recently, in fact, as I was picking up my daughter from an afterschool program, I overheard a dark-skinned black mother loudly chastising her beautifully dark-skinned nine-year-old daughter for getting too much sun exposure. "Look how dark you've gotten," I remember her scolding. "I told you about staying out in the sun so long." From the look of dejection on the girl's face, I could tell that she was embarrassed and ashamed. I can only imagine what kind of emotional damage was done to that beautiful girl's self-esteem that day. Concomitantly, I can only imagine the damage that was done to her mother's thinking that prompted her to say such a thing to someone she clearly loved. Little wonder, then, that comments like "You're pretty for a dark-skinned girl," are still in vogue in black spaces and rarely challenged in the public sphere.

Though it was not the first text to engage such taboo subjects as the politics of colorism for black women, Zora Neale Hurston's *Their Eyes Were Watching God* certainly brought the issue to public consciousness in unprecedented ways. Though Hurston's examination of colorism is not without its problems, which I will turn to below, she exposes a crucial link between colorism and internalized white male supremacy. The novel's indicting portrait of Mrs. Turner (turn her) in the novel – which receives only cursory attention in the scholarship – brings Hurston's writerly critique into focus. A light-skinned proprietor of a bar/restaurant in the Muck, Mrs. Turner befriends the biracial, light-skinned protagonist Janie because of her appearance. Staunch colorist that she is, Mrs. Turner thinks that Janie is too good for her darker-skinned husband, Tea Cake, and openly expresses her disapproval. In fact, she tries to convince Janie to leave Tea Cake and marry her lighter-skinned brother. Hurston exposes the white supremacist thinking undergirding Mrs. Turner's colorist mindset when the narrator reports,

> Mrs. Turner, like all other believers, had built an altar to the unattainable – Caucasian characteristics for all. Her god would smite her, would hurl her from pinnacles and lose her in deserts, but she would not forsake his altars. Behind her crude words was a belief that somehow she and others through worship could attain her paradise – a heaven of straight-haired, thin-lipped, high-nose-boned white seraphs. The physical impossibilities in no way injured faith.[12]

Here, Hurston zeroes in on Mrs. Turner's colorist politics, exposing the white supremacist ideology that Mrs. Turner internalizes as inherently pathological because it prompts blacks to see whiteness as normative and civilized and blackness as deviant and primitive. Mrs. Turner is so blinded by this internalized white supremacy that the absurdity of her pursuit of the biologically unattainable completely escapes her. Indeed, Hurston parodies Mrs. Turner's internalized white supremacy and colorist politics to such a degree that she emerges as a buffoon – someone to be laughed at, scorned, or dismissed as a sellout.

If there is a flaw in Hurston's portrait of Mrs. Turner, it is that Hurston privileges Tea Cake's patriarchal-driven attacks against her. As I note elsewhere, Tea Cake's retaliation against Mrs. Turner in the form of beating Janie bespeaks his feelings of patriarchal entitlement and skewed notions of victimhood.[13] Because Hurston frames the colorist conflict between Tea Cake and Mrs. Turner as a dichotomy – light-skinned elite versus dark-skinned common folk – Tea Cake's abusive patriarchal perspectives and behaviors emerge in the novel as justified, at least to the extent that they apply to light-skinned elite women like Mrs. Turner.

Further complicating matters on this score, the novel romanticizes Tea Cake and working-class black men's gendered investments in white beauty and femininity. When Tea Cake brags to his best friend Sop-de-Bottom about beating Janie to show Mrs. Turner who's boss, Sop-de-Bottom responds playfully with envy. Reflecting black men's gendered investments in white beauty and femininity, Sop-de-Bottom gives Tea Cake props for marrying a woman who both looks and acts the part of hegemonic femininity. We witness Hill Collins's argument that the extant discourse of white beauty depends on a diametrically opposing view of black women as unattractive and unfeminine in the ways that Sop-de-Bottom draws a distinction in femininity between Janie and darker-skinned black women:

> "Tea Cake, yu sho is a lucky man . . . Uh person can see every place you hit her. Ah bet she never raised her hand tuh hit yuh back, neither. Take some uh dese ol' rusty black women and dey would fight yuh all night long and next day nobody couldn't tell you ever hit 'em. Dat's de reason Ah done quit beatin' mah woman. You can't make no mark on 'em at all. Lawd! Wouldn't Ah love tuh whip uh tender woman lak Janie! Ah bet she don't even holler. She jus' cries, eh Tea Cake?"[14]

This scene tells us less about Janie's actual behavior (she not only fights back, as evidenced by the scuffle that she initiates with Tea Cake over infidelity, but she ultimately kills him in self-defense) than it does about Sop-de-Bottom and black men's perceptions of white beauty and ideal womanhood. Tea Cake's dark skin and working-class status operate in this instance to raise his "swag" currency as a playboy. He has managed on charisma and charm alone to land the next best thing to a white woman – a light-skinned wife with substantial assets. Though Janie's behavior does not fit with Sop-de-Bottom's white fantasy and Tea Cake knows as much, Tea Cake cosigns his friend's skewed viewpoint: "Dat's Right."[15] Hurston's narrator even tacitly gives credence to this twisted white fantasy, reporting that both the women and men in the Muck were envious of the way in which Tea Cake and Janie made up the next day after the beating: "The way he petted and pampered her as if those two or three face slaps had nearly killed her made the women see visions and the helpless way she hung on him made the men dream dreams."[16]

Of course, Hurston's decision to have Janie kill a rabidly patriarchal Tea Cake in self-defense demonstrates her awareness of the limitations of his brand of manhood and Janie's attraction/repulsion to it. As stated earlier, Janie does not fit Tea Cake and Sop-de-Bottom's fantasy of white womanhood. Taken from a readerly perspective, it appears that Hurston was grappling with how to demonstrate support for Tea Cake and darker-skinned, working-class black men and, at the same time, empower her feminist-minded female protagonist. What Hurston conveys in the novel is a clear rejection of colorism, as employed by the light-skinned black elite, but a much murkier and more problematic perspective on colorism as it informs working-class black men's notions of gender roles and beauty. However limiting were Hurston's blind spots regarding working-class black men in *Their Eyes*, she clearly recognized that colorism was an extension of white supremacy and thus a major threat to black self-esteem and empowerment. In a word, she was well ahead of the political curve on this issue for her time period.

While Hurston's insights on colorism in *Their Eyes* might not seem all that radical to a contemporary reader, they were nothing short of scandalous in the 1930s when the novel was published. As Hurston jocularly observes in her controversial autobiography *Dust Tracks on a Road*, the stigmas against dark skin were so intense in the post–Reconstruction era that black folks often claimed Indian ancestry to distance themselves from blackness. Clearly proud of her racial heritage, Hurston asserts, "I saw no curse in being black, nor no extra flavor by being white. I saw no benefit in excusing my looks by claiming to be half Indian. In fact, I boast that I am the only Negro in the United States whose grandfather on the mother's side was not an Indian chief."[17] Even as Hurston's pro-black impulse in *Dust Tracks* is tempered, if not undercut, by her seeming willingness to let whites off the hook for creating and perpetuating colorism, it nevertheless flies in the face of racial common sense in an era that linked whiteness to beauty, status, and prestige.[18] While scholars typically invoke Hurton's feminist impulse in the novel to explain why many of her black contemporaries, like Richard Wright, sought to silence and/or discredit her[19] (Wright notoriously maligned *Their Eyes* as carrying "no theme, no message, no thought"),[20] her unapologetic attack on colorism was undoubtedly a motivating factor as well.

Hurston's *Their Eyes* is also instructive because it shines light – consciously and unconsciously – on the crucial role black men play in perpetuating normative white beauty. Conditioned to see lighter-skinned women as one step down on the social ladder, below white women (who were largely off-limits to black men, legally and otherwise, until the latter part of the twentieth century), black men actively pursued them as lovers and wives. *Their Eyes* suggests that elite black men like Joe Starks are the chief culprits of this colorist patriarchal mindset, but the reality is that the Tea Cakes of the world were just as complicit. Because light skin and class status were often tied together (the unspoken mandate among the elite being to lighten up the race), it meant that darker-skinned men were at a marked disadvantage when it came to dating and marrying lighter-skinned women unless they had something else going for them, such as wealth, prestige, or celebrity.

Chester Himes's protagonist Bob Jones exemplifies this colorist thinking in *If He Hollers Let Him Go*. Looking to rise in social stature, Bob Jones pursues and becomes engaged to a middle-class black woman who is light enough to pass as white. Though he revels in the social currency that he receives in society for having such a "prized" woman on his hip, he is also frustrated by the fact that her status and white beauty prevent him from controlling and dominating her as he is accustomed to doing with his darker-skinned girlfriends/conquests. Tea Cake's "pampering" of Janie after he smacks her around in the name of teaching Mrs. Turner a lesson is premised on the same gendered mindset. Tea Cake's conversation with Sop-de-Bottom following the beating leaves no doubt that Janie's white beauty and class status radically informed Tea Cake's "deferential" behavior towards her.

Further evidence of black men's twisted investment in white beauty and femininity can be found in George Schuyler's satirical novel *Black No More*. Schuyler cast light on this phenomenon in the ways he parodies the colorist politics of the black elite generally and black elite men in particular. More specifically, he illuminates the hypocrisy of African American male leaders at the turn of the twentieth century who espoused black agendas and claimed to love black folks but were staunch colorists, marrying and employing only lighter-skinned women. When a machine is invented that allows blacks to become white, the black leaders rail against it in the name of preserving and celebrating blackness, even though their real motivation – as demonstrated by their colorist preferences and behaviors – is to preserve their jobs not challenge normative whiteness. In an obvious parody of iconic black leader W. E. B. Du Bois, Schuyler writes, "Like most Negro leaders, he deified the black woman but abstained from employing aught save octoroons. He talked at white banquets about 'we of the black race' and admitted in books that he was part-French, part-Russian, part-Indian and part-Negro. He bitterly denounced the Nordics for debauching Negro women while taking care to hire comely yellow stenographers with weak resistance. In a real way, he loved his people."[21]

This colorist bias emerges too in Ralph Ellison's *Invisible Man,* albeit in a way that perpetuates it rather than exposing it as a problem. We witness this dynamic when the young male protagonist in his "pre-invisible" days aspires to be like Mr. Bledsoe, the assimilated president of his college. Among the things that most impress invisible man about Mr. Bledsoe beyond his wealth, influence, and power is his "good-looking and creamy complexioned wife."[22] Though Mr. Bledsoe's stock as a role model plummets in invisible man's eyes the more he becomes politically enlightened, the issue of Mr. Bledsoe's choice of a "creamy complexioned" wife is never at issue in the protagonist's mind or the novel. Indeed, what little attention Ellison pays to women's subjectivity in *Invisible Man* revolves mostly around white women.[23]

Though her novel is primarily concerned with the effects of colorist politics on the self-esteem and the political consciousness of black girls,

Morrison's *The Bluest Eye* provides key insights into black boys' unconscious complicity in normative white beauty. The scene that comes immediately to mind is when sisters Claudia and Frieda intervene to defend
their friend Pecola Breedlove, who is a poor, dark-skinned girl, from a
group of young male bullies. Pecola's dark skin coupled with her unstable
family situation make her an easy target for boys conditioned to scorn
the version of blackness that Pecola embodies. They display their scorn
with chants of "Black e mo. Black e mo. Yadaddsleepsnekked." Morrison
delineates their mindset:

> They had extemporized a verse made up of two insults about matters over which
> the victim had no control: the color of her skin and speculations on the sleeping
> habits of an adult, wildly fitting in its incoherence. That they themselves were
> black, or that their own father had similarly relaxed habits, was irrelevant. It was
> their contempt for their own blackness that gave the first insult its teeth. They
> seemed to have taken all of their smoothly cultivated ignorance, their exquisitely
> learned self-hatred, their elaborately designed hopelessness and sucked it all
> up into a fiery cone of scorn that had burned for ages in the hollows of their
> minds – cooled – and spilled over lips of outrage, consuming whatever was in
> their path. They danced a macabre ballet around the victim, whom, for their own
> sake, they were prepared to sacrifice to the flaming pit.[24]

Turning the critical lens back onto Pecola's bullies, Morrison reveals that
the boys' venom against Pecola is radically displaced. What they despise
about Pecola's blackness is what they have been socially conditioned to
despise about themselves. Morrison's striking word choice in describing this programming – "smoothly cultivated ignorance," "exquisitely
learned self-hatred," and "elaborately designed hopelessness" – bespeaks
the tenacity and insidiousness of this conditioning. Lacking a critical
discourse to bring these feelings of self-hate and hopelessness to the
fore, the boys collapse into attack mode and use Pecola as an emotional
punching bag. We witness how this social conditioning shapes the black
boys' perceptions of white beauty when Maureen Peal – the popular
and well-to-do light-skinned girl – arrives on the scene and sidles up to
Frieda, who is holding on to Pecola. Frieda reports: "Maureen appeared
at my elbow, and the boys seemed reluctant to continue under her spring-
time eyes so wide with interest. They buckled in confusion, not willing to
beat up three girls under her watchful gaze. So they listened to a budding
male instinct that told them to pretend we were unworthy of their atten-

tion."[25] The embodiment of light skin privilege and beauty, Maureen's seeming support of Frieda and Claudia's intervention is enough to send the boys into retreat. Maureen symbolizes the kind of girl that most of them have been taught to praise and pursue, and they don't want to risk looking foolish in her eyes. What Morrison reveals later in the scene is that Maureen's racial mindset is as skewed as the boys who bully Pecola. This empowers Frieda and Claudia – who are at once envious of and frustrated by all the attention Maureen receives because of her white beauty – to unload on her emotionally. In the final analysis, however, they rightly recognize that Maureen is a victim of internalized white supremacy as well: "All the time [we were trading insults with her] we knew that Maureen Peal was not the Enemy and not worthy of such intense hatred. The *Thing* to fear was the *Thing* that made her beautiful, and not us."[26]

The sad truth is that as a society we have not moved substantially beyond the standards of white normative beauty described in *The Bluest Eye,* which was set in the 1930s. In the 1990s, when I was an undergraduate in college, black men routinely referred to desirable light-skinned girls as "red bones." If a black man had a "red bone" girlfriend who was also "thick" and curvy he was considered a lucky man indeed. Though this colorist dynamic has been at play throughout my entire life, I can scarcely remember having a critical conversation about the cultural currency of skin tone with any of my black male peers. Which is not to say that the issue of skin tone wasn't a hot topic; it certainly was. The reality is that it was assumed a priori that women with normative white features were more attractive than darker-skinned black women with Afrocentric features. Dark-skinned girls thought to be attractive were treated as aberrations, exceptions to the rule, so to speak, of normative white beauty. Comments of the sort that the aforementioned dark-skinned teacher recalls receiving from men about her beauty – "you're attractive for a dark sista" – were commonly voiced with impunity in black spaces. Darker skin for black women was also tethered to unfeminine and socially undesirable behavior. What this usually meant on the dating scene was that black men typically did not extend darker-skinned black girls the same level of respect as white girls or lighter-skinned black girls. The pecking order of beauty was dramatically on display among the black sororities. The two most popular sororities – and thus hardest ones to get into – were largely comprised of lighter-skinned women. The less popular ones were largely comprised of darker-skinned women and comparatively easier to join. Spike Lee's highly controversial 1988 film *School Daze* tackled this phenomenon on college campuses. What the movie made clear was that the colorist politics Hurston was grappling with in the 1930s were still radically informing black notions of beauty and status at the end of the century.

Let me add here, to echo Tracy Sharpley-Whiting's insights in *Pimps Up, Ho's Down: Hip Hop's Hold on Young Black Women,* that despite this investment in white beauty, black men have long valued curvy, full-figured black women, as evidenced by popular songs like the Commodores 1977 hit "Brick House" and such songs of my high school and college days as E.U.'s 1988 hit "Doing the Butt" and Sir Mix A Lot's 1992 smash single "Baby Got Back." We see the colorist limitations of this celebration of black women's bodies, however, in songs like rapper Nelly's "Tip Drill." For the uninitiated, a "tip drill" in hip hop culture is the act during sex of tipping a black women with a "nice" body but "ugly" face over doggy style, the idea being that this sexual position allows the man to avoid having to look at the woman's face during sex and thus being turned off. The hook to the song says it all: "It must be ya ass cause it ain't ya face / I need a tip drill, I need a tip drill."[27] In the video Nelly infamously slides a credit card down the crack of one of the video actresses' derriere like it was an ATM. Given the colorist politics that continue to inform heterosexual black men's sexual preferences, the black women that fall into this category of tip drill candidates will surely be dark-skinned with Afrocentric features. Thus, even though black men in the contemporary era can be credited with celebrating nontraditional body types in black women,[28] this celebration is often complicated by extant investments in white beauty. Sharpley-Whiting explains that this preference for white beauty and femininity and black women's "thickness" has collapsed into a fetishization of ethnically mixed women. She observes that the ideal woman in twenty-first–century black hip hop culture is "black-derived, curvy, and 'thick,' but she is 'paprika'd' and salted with difference, as with the October 2004 Black-Irish-Cherokee-Asian 'Eye Candy' centerfold in the hip hop magazine XXL, or December 2004's African-American-

Egyptian-Brazilian 'Eye Candy' spread. Beginning at the opposite ends of the great chain of beauty's color spectrum, hip hop culture and mainstream meet somewhere in the middle in their fetishization of ethnic brewing."[29] In this "great chain of beauty's color spectrum," then, little has changed for dark-skinned black girls and women; they remain at the opposite of end from whiteness and beauty.

Though I am certainly encouraged by the fact that there is more of an awareness about such issues of black women's beauty than there was, say, just twenty years ago, when wearing locs for a woman was a major fashion faux pas, I think that we have a lot further to go than many of us are willing to admit. Consider a recent internet video that went viral featuring two white teenage Santaluces High School (Florida) girls who fit the normative white beauty profile, bashing their black peers. The girls reserve their harshest attacks for black girls, whom they malign for doing everything within their power to accommodate normative white beauty standards, including putting in hair weave. At one point, in fact, the two girls start flinging and brushing their hair in mockery, making remarks like "I feel sorry for black girls because they can't brush their hair like this" and "They've got to pat dat weave to keep it in place."[30] Even though the video has sparked public outcry and the girls have been disciplined by their school, I think it would be shortsighted to see their perspectives as isolated and insignificant. However racist are their perspectives, what these white teenagers witness on television, the internet, magazines, and in their lived experience are many young black girls and women striving for normative white beauty; striving desperately to look like them.

Because normative white beauty is so hardwired into our racial consciousness, even well-meaning attempts to combat it can fall flat. I am reminded here of the efforts by Fro-lific to empower black girls. The Georgia-based group gained national notoriety for giving away black Barbie dolls to underprivileged black girls. To underscore the importance of celebrating black women's physical characteristics, Fro-lific nappied up the Barbies' hair using boiling water and pipe cleaners. While this gesture is certainly a step in the right direction, it hardly explodes the image of white beauty. As Martha Pitts writes in her op-ed "Happy-To-Be-Nappy Barbie":

One might assume that Fro-lific's implied goal of teaching the girls self-love and
self-acceptance should make me, a black mother of a black daughter, stand up
and cheer like everyone else seems to be doing... right? But here's the thing:
As a feminist mom, I kinda hate Barbie, whatever her color. In fact, I would go
so far as to say that Barbie represents everything I hate in the world: capitalism,
sexism, racism, heteronormativity, white supremacy.

How does black Barbie reinforce white supremacy, you ask? Well, first, look at
her facial features and body shape. Remind you of anyone?[31]

Pitts invokes Ann Ducille's 1994 essay "Dyes and Dolls: Multicul-
tural Barbie and the Merchandising of Difference" to make the case
that black women cannot trust a capitalistic enterprise such as a doll
manufacturer "to produce a line of doll that would more fully reflect the
wide variety of sizes, shapes, colors, hairstyles, occupations, abilities, and
disabilities that African Americans – like all people – come in."[32] Pitts
argues that this is a central question Fro-lific and black women should
be thinking about whether or not they continue to give black girls Barbie
dolls. Pitt concludes, "Barbie may be too pervasive [for black women] to
ignore, but at least the dolls can be a starting point for important discussions about black girlhood. . . . Can we question Barbie's big breasts and
tiny waist as markers of True Womanhood? Why is Ken Barbie's significant other? Why do these black Barbies have to wear Jay-Z's 'Rocawear'
clothing line?"[33]

Pitts's reservations about Fro-lific's well-intentioned but problematic efforts for black girls' empowerment underscore why black girls and
women cannot rely on corporate America to intervene on such issues.
Take Disney's "Princess and the Frog," for example. Despite the fact that
Disney has long been one of the most egregious perpetrators of racist
black stereotypes and xenophobia, many blacks flocked to support the
movie with little or no regard for the political implications of this history. A blog post comment by a black woman, "Jami," about the racial
politics surrounding "The Princess and the Frog" is indicative of the
uncritical black celebration of the movie: "I'm sure there are some African Americans out there that will not be completely satisfied until they
see an African-American princess with an afro, braids, dreads; a broad
nose; big lips; large thighs and wide hips. . . . Yes, it's hard to please our
people sometimes. However, I'm sure that many feel that the [movie] . . .
was a good start."[34] This blogger erroneously misreads an appeal (like

Pitts's) for more inclusiveness and diverse representations of black girls' and women's beauty as being overly demanding. One also gets the sense from this blogger's comments that a black princess with non-Eurocentric features – like an Afrocentric nose and full lips – would be unappealing. Though white women enjoy a much broader and more diverse representation of white womanhood on the big screen than do black women, the blogger identifies "hard to please" blacks as the problem, not the white-dominated and historically racist Hollywood industry. The survivors of demeaning white stereotypical portraits get blamed for their own marginalization.

The recent movie *Something New,* starring Sanaa Lathan as Kenya McQueen and Simon Baker as Brian Kelly, delivers a similar problematic message about normative white beauty and black women. An interracial love story that recalls the white liberal paternalistic movie *Guess Who's Coming to Dinner,* the movie displaces the problem of normative white beauty onto upper class and snooty blacks. Moreover, the movie characterizes the strikingly handsome, nature-loving, affable white gardener as an Everyman figure who has a valuable and universal lesson about self-love to teach Kenya and black women. Indeed, Brian is the chief reason that Kenya abandons her hair weave and goes natural. White men – the historical orchestrators of normative white beauty and black women's inferiority – emerge via the character of Brian as liberators of black women's consciousness. In effect, it takes the white man to teach black women how to love themselves and be proud of their bodies. To this extent, the white paternalistic impulse of the movie rivals that of *Guess Who's Coming to Dinner,* the major difference being that *Something New* was directed by a woman of color, Sanaa Hamri, and widely celebrated in black spaces. Both the lead actress, Sanaa Lathan, and director Hamri were nominated for NAACP Image awards.

The truth of the matter is that normative white beauty is alive and well. In order to combat it, black folks are going to have to remain politically vigilant and refuse to allow white male supremacy to dictate the terms upon which we value how we look, behave, and think. As Pitts astutely points out, accomplishing this goal is no easy task, because the discourse of normative whiteness is so intense and pervasive that even when we try to challenge it, as the Fro-lific group attempts to do by giving black girls afro-ed Barbies, we often end up perpetuating it.

Extant taboos against discussing such matters in the public domain mean that those of us willing to speak out against these debilitating beauty standards for black girls and women will most definitely encounter conflict in and beyond black spaces. My run-in with my daughter's kindergarten teacher certainly bears out this reality. The most valuable lesson I learned from the encounter was that I have to take an even larger role in educating my daughter about self-worth and empowering her with a critical model to navigate the tricky social terrain of normative white beauty. My first step toward this goal was to sit down with Octavia one-on-one to explain why I was so adamant against her dressing as Goldilocks for the book parade. I ended our discussion by telling Octavia that I thought she was smart, beautiful, and talented just the way she was. As soon as the words left my lips, Octavia's face lit up as if she'd just been offered a bowl of strawberries, her favorite treat. It was simply the most beautiful thing in the world to see. While I'm not sure – beyond writing this chapter – how best to go about tackling this mammoth issue of normative white beauty that has taken such a serious toll on black girls' self-image and self-esteem, I know with certainty that there will be at least one less black girl on this earth who will feel the need to look like Goldilocks in order to be beautiful.

Look at you. You black, you pore, you ugly, you
a woman. Goddam, he say, you nothing at all.

Mr. _____ attacking Celie in
Alice Walker's *The Color Purple*

"Stop Making the Rest of Us Look Bad": How Class Matters in the Attacks against the Movie *Precious*

WHEN THE MOVIE *PRECIOUS* DEBUTED IN 2009 MANY BLACK folks in high places viewed it as an abomination, a twenty-first-century brand of black poverty tourism. Indeed, one of the movie's most vocal and esteemed antagonists then was Ishmael Reed, who launched a virtual campaign against the movie, going so far as to cast the movie's black producers, screenwriter, director, and actors as modern-day Uncle Toms, willing to sell their black souls for a slice of fame and at the direct expense of perpetuating black stereotypes. Not surprisingly, in the public arena (which means, of course, that white folks are listening in) the discussion over the movie collapsed into a pro/con debate on whether blacks should celebrate or disavow it. Given that two of the most popular black folks on the planet, Oprah Winfrey and Tyler Perry, signed on as executive producers of the movie, the pro-*Precious* camp definitely won the public relations war. It also helped that black fan favorite actress/comedian, Mo'Nique walked away with an Oscar for best supporting actress (only the fifth black woman in history to be so honored) and screenwriter Geoffrey Fletcher became the first African American to win in the category of Best Adapted Screenplay.

Sidestepping this pro/con debate on the movie, in this chapter I will examine the various race and class implications of this movie, and also discuss how white surveillance continues to alter the ways that blacks react to whites and each other. While it is still the case that many blacks prefer to keep the taboo portraits of blackness that *Precious* broaches out of the public eye, including that of impoverished blacks gaming the welfare/workfare system, abusing their children (emotionally and sexually), and self-destructing in about every way imaginable, my contention is that the mental, emotional, and spiritual health of our communities is bound up in being able to air our dirty laundry. Lest my prescriptions be misunderstood, this airing of dirty laundry is not simply about taking personal responsibility and owning up to the black communities' social failings; it is also about speaking openly and frankly about the ways that whites benefit directly and indirectly from age-old white privilege, fueling the socioeconomic fires that are at least partly to blame for the tragic black realities on display in the film. However uncomfortable discussing many of these subjects might make some blacks feel, the real danger resides socially in shutting down these avenues of artistic-political expression in the name of black respectability, strategic solidarity, and combating black stereotypes rather than in opening them up.

Though *Precious* is usefully controversial in all the ways I have outlined above, it is neither fair nor productive to dismiss the movie's detractors out of hand. And, here, let's start with a brief discussion of the racial receptivity of the novel *PUSH* by Sapphire (Ramona Lofton) upon which the movie is based. While the novel has enjoyed a diverse readership – at least along racial lines – it has been elevated to the pinnacle of black "realness" by a noticeably white and paternalistic body of readers that cut across political lines. To be more precise, these readers treat the unique and intersecting race, gender, and class experiences of the protagonist Precious as a reflection of *authentic* black experience. Purportedly, what makes Precious's experiences of blackness more "authentic" than, say, my own rural-black-working-class-cum-black-middle-class-existence is that hers more closely reflects paternalistic whites' view of blacks as poor, downtrodden, pathological, and tragic. (The white receptivity of recent blockbuster movies *The Blind Side* and *The Help*, which far outperformed *Precious* at the box office, operate upon a similar paternalistic impulse.) I'm reminded here of white critic Irving Howe's warped assertion that Richard Wright's *Native Son* (which featured the ruthless ghetto dweller and madman Bigger Thomas) was more "black" and "authentic" than Ralph Ellison's *Invisible Man* (which featured a near-polar opposite protagonist in the highly philosophical and intellectual invisible man). Failing to extend to blacks the same level of complexity with which he engaged white consciousness and humanity, the paternalistic

Howe dismissed Ellison's characterization of his black protagonist as too brainy and introspective to be believable. Ellison writes, "Howe makes of 'Negroness' a metaphysical condition, one that is a state of irremediable agony which all but engulfs the mind. Happily the view from inside the skin is not so dark as it appears to be from Howe's remote [white] position . . ."[1] From Howe's (not so critical) perspective, real black men teetered always on the edge of violence and obsessed over white oppression even to the point of self-destruction. Thus, even in Howe's genuine attempt to legitimize black suffering via Wright's novel and portrait of Thomas, he exhibited his white privilege and bias, essentially telling Ellison, a black man and thinker of the first order, that he – a white man – was better qualified to determine what was and wasn't authentic blackness.

To bring the issue closer to home, several years back I witnessed an indignant white undergraduate female student at the University of Wisconsin–Madison try to blast my mentor, the late Dr. Nellie McKay, in the hall for using the term "mulatto" during an in-class discussion to describe multiracial characters in Nella Larson's novella *Passing*. Apparently, the white student had learned from an African American history course she was taking at the time – which, as it happened, was being taught by a white male professor, Timothy Tyson[2] – that the term "mulatto" was deeply offensive to blacks. The student felt that in using the term McKay was perpetuating black inferiority, if not completely selling out the race. This theater of the racially absurd was put to a dramatic end when one of McKay's black female graduate students who overheard the discussion stepped in and checked the white girl on her white privilege run amok. When the white girl retreated in tears, saying that she didn't intend to be insulting, McKay's graduate student explained to the white student that her "good intentions" plea did not resolve her of racial culpability. Racial paternalism assumes white supremacy/black inferiority. This phenomenon explains why this white student – who was reared in an all-white environment in the Midwest and had taken just one class in African American history her entire life – felt empowered to chastise a black women and premier scholar of African American literature. (Dr. McKay, by the way, never intervened. My guess is that she was either exasperated beyond words with such racial tomfoolery – which was/is not unusual in Madison, or at most universities, for that matter – or she felt that her graduate student had put the matter to rest.)

As for how such issues of white paternalism converge with intraracial class elitism/colorism and "UncleTom-ism" in the receptivity of *Precious,* there is perhaps no better starting point for analysis than Percival Everett's irreverent satire *Erasure.* Published in 2001, *Erasure* anticipated, if not forecasted, the 2009 debate that erupted around the movie *Precious. Erasure* features a frustrated writer and college professor, Thelonius "Monk" Ellison, who becomes infuriated by the fact that a novel called *We's Lives in Da Ghetto* by Juanita Mae Jenkins (thinly veiled references to PUSH and author Sapphire) becomes a best-seller, secures a lucrative movie deal, and turns Jenkins into a celebrity. In protest, Monk, a prolific writer of intellectually dense novels that don't sell very well, writes his own version of a "ghetto" novel (rewriting Richard Wright's *Native Son* as "street lit" to highlight white blindness to black diversity and humanity), titled *My Pafology* and then later renamed *Fuck.*

Though Monk – an elitist who comes from a well-heeled family – writes the novel as a satire to protest whites' pathological obsession with black stereotypes, he has his agent present the novel to publishers as realism. In a twist reminiscent of Spike Lee's *Bamboozled,* the political experiment backfires and the novel takes off, making Monk – who writes under the pen name Stagg R. Leigh – a millionaire and celebrity, like his writerly nemesis Jenkins. Intoxicated by the fame even as he is mortified by his resemblance to Jenkins, Monk carves out a gangsta identity under his pen name, playing upon the stereotypical expectations of his mostly white fan base and publisher. To assuage feelings of selling out, he thinks of himself as a kind of modern day trickster, cashing in on whites' twisted preoccupation with "imagined" black pathologies. His mind game explodes, however, when he is selected as the only black judge on a highly prestigious book award panel and his novel becomes the top choice of the white judges. Terrified that his novel will win, expose his protest-turned-shoddy-scheme, and become yet another minstrel enterprise for white consumption, Monk maligns the novel as "offensive, poorly written, racist and mindless."[3] Rather than take Monk's criticisms to heart, his white colleagues and fellow judges respond with disbelief and indignation. One judge opines, "This is the truest novel I've ever read. It could only have been written by someone who has done hard time. It's the real thing." Another judge remarks to Monk, "I would think you'd be happy to have the story of *your* people so vividly portrayed."[4]

Encapsulating the extent to which whites distort black realities to line up with their expectations of black pathology, Monk's insider cultural perspective as an African American has little or no bearing on how the paternalistic white committee members vote. In fact, similar to the white girl who verbally attacked Dr. McKay, the white committee members lambaste Monk on the basis of what they perceive as *his* warped racial conscious. In the end, white perceptions of black realities trump the perceptions and lived experiences of the "actual" black person in the room. "That's democracy," Monk jokes sardonically when the committee votes overwhelmingly and along racial lines to award the literary prize to the novel *Fuck*.[5] The joke, of course, is that though everyone on the committee gets an equal opportunity to vote, by virtue of being outnumbered and overpowered, the "black vote" becomes inconsequential to the ultimate outcome. Hip to his complicity in perpetuating these racial narratives (after all, he did willfully take the payoff for his novel and play the part of gangsta-cum-novelist), Monk reflects that he was a victim of racism precisely because he strove to be postracial and, in doing so, underestimated the tenacity of "race" in America. More specifically, he underestimated the power of whites to dictate the social and economic terms upon which blacks determine their social value and gauge "realness." His trickster hustle – exploiting white expectations of black inferiority for cash – ultimately served to strengthen the status quo. The joke, as it turns out, ended up being on him, as he wore "the [racial] mask of the person I was expected to be" despite a desire to expose white racial hypocrisy and blacks' willful and unconscious participation in it.[6]

My suspicion is that those who see *Precious* as racist propaganda or poverty tourism view it in the same light as Monk does – or at least did – the novel *We's Live in Da Ghetto* by Jenkins. They know that a racial calculus still exists in the America whereby blacks who act in accordance with racial stereotypes – especially in the field of entertainment – are, at times, handsomely rewarded. To understand this dynamic is to understand why, after a bit of political soul-searching at the height of their popularity, Richard Pryor stopped using the word "nigger" to describe black folks in his standup routines and Dave Chappelle walked away from his hit show and a fifty-million-dollar payday. Or, on the flipside, why one-time Public Enemy hook-meister William Drayton's (aka Flava Flav) minstrelsy persona and stint on the reality TV circuit has significantly increased his celebrity status and bank account.

This "get-paid-to-denigrate-blackness" calculus was, in fact, at the heart of an iconic speech, "Criteria of Negro Art," delivered at the NAACP conference in Chicago by the venerable intellectual W. E. B. Du Bois nearly a century ago. Du Bois argued that all "art is [racial] propaganda,"[7] and that it was thus the duty of "responsible" black artists to create art that depicted blacks in a flattering light to counteract stereotypical white portraits. He also characterized the money and publicity that a handful of black artists were receiving at the time from white philanthropists and publishers as "subtle and deadly bribes," designed to seduce the younger black writers into believing that racism was passé and that a new day of racial equality was on the horizon.[8]

What Du Bois makes clear here and, indeed, Everett maps out brilliantly in *Erasure*, is that it is naive and dangerous to ignore the degree to which white perceptions of blackness influence how we're viewed on a global scale and, more importantly, how we view each other at national and local levels. The problem, as it were, emerges in the solution-development stage. In *Erasure* Monk tries to explode this racial calculus initially by shaming whites – throwing their twisted images of blacks back at them to highlight their warped racial superiority complex. In the end, however, he emerges as little more than a white supremacy enabler. Part of the reason that he finds himself in this predicament is that he never fully comes to terms with his investment in pleasing whites (i.e., measuring up to their prescribed and raced standards of excellence) and his not-so-subtle contempt for poor and lowdown black folk, especially black women. Everett reveals that, at bottom, Monk is as compromised racially and politically as he imagines his nemesis Jenkins to be. I say "imagines" because the reader is privy only to Monk's biased perceptions of her feelings and motivations as a writer.

In many regards we also need to be wary of Du Bois's class and race politics, at least to the extent to which he agitates for black artists to create more flattering images of black folks. Quiet as it's kept, Du Bois – who created the concept of "The Talented Tenth," which asserted that black uplift depended on the educated and elite 10 percent of the black population to lead the way – harbored more than a little contempt for the lowdown folks as well. While certainly radical in his sociologically grounded attacks against claims of scientific racism and white supremacy (i.e., environment rather than race explains blacks' underachievement and social crises), he nevertheless adapted certain elements of eugenics-thinking (the idea of selective breeding as a way to improve the species) when it came to black social empowerment. Among his most controversial statements to this effect, he argued that "the most intelligent class" of blacks was using too much birth control, while "the mass of ignorant Negroes still breed carelessly and disastrously."[9] Translation: the wrong kinds of black folks are reproducing at much higher rates than the right kind of black folks, making it difficult for blacks as a whole to rise above the social and economic constraints of institutionalized racism. The formula for black uplift boiled down, in part at least, to there being too many Pookies and Preciouses running around, and far too few Baracks and Michelles to mount a successful challenge to the status quo.

Hidden beneath the surface of a very legitimate argument about the movie *Precious* and the problems of white consumption and perpetuation of black stereotypes, is an intraracial class bias, à la Du Bois's talented tenth politics, that holds the poor black masses chiefly responsible for "keeping the race down." The dark-skinned sharecropper turned prominent physician in James Weldon Johnson's *Autobiography of an Ex-Colored Man* captures this racial sentiment precisely when, walking the streets of Washington, D.C., at the turn of the century, he opines:

> You see those lazy, loafing, good-for-nothing darkies; they're not worth digging graves for; yet they are the ones who create impressions of the race for the casual [white] observer. It's because they are always in evidence on the street corners, while the rest of us are hard at work, and you know a dozen loafing darkies make a bigger crowd and a worse impression in this country than fifty white men of the same class. But they ought not to represent the race. We are the race, and the race ought to be judged by us, not by them. Every race and every nation should be judged by the best it has been able to produce, not the worst.[10]

Close scrutiny of this passage reveals the twisted black logic of race and class that continues to inform and complicate similar debates in the twenty-first century. The rags-to-riches black physician is clearly trying to stress the fact that the majority of black folks are hardworking citizens, not the stereotypical "good-for-nothing darkies" that whites make them out to be. The obvious problem here is that the physician slips into a version of blaming blacks for white oppression by hoisting responsibility for the existence of these stereotypes onto poor black folks. That is, rather than account for how whites have historically forced and cemented blacks into socially and economically subordinate status, the physician takes aim at the victims in poor black folks.

The most salient evidence that remnants of this poor-black-folks-are-making-us-look-bad thinking remains with us today is, of course, Bill Cosby's explosive comments at the NAACP banquet celebrating the fiftieth anniversary of the landmark *Brown v. Board of Education* case. He infamously invoked an analogy of a poor black child gunned down by the police for stealing a pound cake to make a point about failed black parenting and squandered opportunities for social advancement by the black poor. If those lowdown black folks would become more responsible and contributing citizens, Cosby's thinking goes, then they wouldn't be stealing in the first place and, by extension, getting gunned down by the police. As the classed biases of Cosby's comments have been roundly critiqued – most notably in Michael Eric Dyson's *Is Bill Cosby Right? Or Has the Black Middle Class Lost Its Mind?* – I will not rehearse the arguments here. It is worth pointing out, however, that several prominent blacks came to Cosby's defense, including Ward Connerly, John H. McWhorter, Cornel West, and Dave Chappelle. What's more, not only did Cosby's bankable and pristine image as a (postracial) role model for parenting and ethical living remain firmly intact, he was touted in many circles – in and beyond the black community – as a heroic figure. Seizing on the momentum, he wrote a bestselling book on the matter – co-authored by esteemed scholar Alvin F. Poussaint – and launched a high-profile town hall meeting–style campaign on black parenting and social responsibility.

Cosby's mass appeal demonstrates the difficulty of uncoupling black strategies of uplift from conditioned, white male supremacist images of blackness and *intra*racial class/caste biases. What this dynamic demands of African Americans, then, relative to evaluating the movie *Precious,* is close scrutiny of how white surveillance influences the ways blacks generally, and the black middle class in particular, react to unflattering portraits of blackness put to art. Indeed, one of the young artists to which Du Bois was directing his fire in his speech, Langston Hughes, fired off his own salvo in "The Negro Artist and the Racial Mountain," basically signaling to Du Bois and his ilk that black artists would not stand for having the political terms of their artistry dictated by anyone, including paternalistic whites or elitist blacks. More specifically, Hughes railed against the idea that the so-called lowdown black folk culture was an embarrassment and, concomitantly, that the key to racial uplift was to draw a clear distinction in the public (white) eye between the lowdown folks and "upstanding Negroes." Rather than play by the prescribed rules of racial respectability – which contributed, in Hughes's eyes, to black artists longing to be white and, conversely, despising their blackness – he beckoned black artists to reflect all facets of blacks' complex humanity in their work, including the unflattering parts, the "tom-tom cries and the tom-tom laughs."[11]

No stranger to intraracial class snobbery, Hughes's working-class mother was once invited and then conspicuously uninvited to attend a posh cultural event sponsored by an elite black Washington club that was to feature her son reading his poetry. The reason the invitation was rescinded had to do with the fear of the club that Mrs. Hughes did not own a proper evening gown. What Hughes knew firsthand, then, was that the propaganda model for black uplift was driven at turns by the black elites' shame and contempt toward lowdown, working-class black folks. Though certainly guilty of a one-size-fits-all indictment of the black intelligentsia and class elites, Hughes usefully flips the black respectability script, casting as the real sellouts to the race those black artists who wanted to distance themselves from blackness and be judged by whites according to their merits. Hidden beneath these lofty appeals for meritocracy, respectability, and universality, Hughes argued, was a desire on the part of black elites to please and be accepted by whites. Freedom for Hughes thus resided in exploding the white terms of evaluating black identity and art, not in accommodating those terms and displacing blame for stereotypes on the most victimized group in working-class blacks. Black respectability and racial propaganda be damned.

If we fast-forward to the twenty-first century and the heated debates within black America about the movie *Precious,* it becomes clear that the "art-as-propaganda" thinking still has cultural currency, especially among the middle-class gatekeepers of black respectability. At the extreme end of this political camp reside Armond White and Ishmael Reed, both of whom liken *Precious* to the vitriolic 1915 racist blockbuster *The Birth of a Nation,* which cast Klansmen as heroic figures and newly emancipated blacks as white-women-raping savages. Firing the first shot, White opines, "Not since *The Birth of a Nation* has a mainstream movie demeaned the idea of black American life as much as *Precious.*"[12] Not to be outdone, Reed takes White's outlandish comparison even further, noting in *Counterpunch* that "Precious" makes the racist director of *The Birth of a Nation,* D. W. Griffith, "look like a progressive."[13] What we see on display in their extraordinary likening of *Precious* to *The Birth of a Nation* is the extent to which they are considering what whites – specifically those on the Right who use stereotypical black portraits to displace blame for racial inequalities onto blacks – will take away from the movie. Indeed, Reed highlights the fact that former First Lady Barbara Bush strongly endorsed the movie, along with a host of other paternalistic whites with questionable political motives.

What bleeds through Armond and Reed's reviews, however, is more than just resentment toward the cadre of blacks involved in the writing, producing, directing, and acting in the movie. Collectively, they exhibit a striking, if politically coded, contempt for the kinds of black folks represented in the film. Both take aim, for example, at the physical appearance of Gabourey Sidibe, the actress portraying Precious. With telling irony, Armond – who blasts the movie for casting the most redeeming black characters as light-skinned – refers to Sidibe being so obese and "animal-like" in her portrayal that "her face seems bloated into a permanent pout."[14] Following along a similar path of argumentation, Reed characterizes the *New York Times Magazine* cover photo of Sidibe – whom he describes pejoratively and repeatedly as "the 350-pound actor in the title role" – as "an act of black exploitation."[15] Though Reed – an avid reader and prolific writer – underscores his claim of an advertising conspiracy by chronicling the admittedly torrid history of the magazine's representation of poor black women, he becomes guilty of reproducing a version of those representations in his transparent distaste for Sidibe's physical appearance. We see Reed's true motives as it concerns poor black women's suffering in his mind-boggling suggestion, citing a comment by writer Cecil Brown, that the real victim in the movie is Carl, Precious's pedophile father, who impregnates her twice, and black men as a whole, who are the preferred scapegoats for all things wrong with American society, including the social degradation of black women. So adamant is his defense of black men as scapegoats for white America generally, and feminists (black and white) specifically, that he completely ignores black men's agency, as if all of our destructive behaviors are directly contributable to white oppression. Presumably, then, *Precious* was unfair to Carl and, by extension, black (straight) men (Reed draws direct links between director Lee Daniels's queerness, coziness with whites, and his depiction of straight black men) because it failed to account for the institutional white forces that corrupted his and black men's humanity. Interestingly enough, when Mark Anthony Neal, Nicholas Powers, and I pushed back against Reed's black nationalist patriarchal thinking on *Precious* in various blogs and social media outlets, he responded with venom, questioning not just our support of black feminism and the movie, but our very manhood.[16]

Reed's gatekeeper status aside, a common denominator in the anti-*Precious* arguments is that the movie grossly distorts black realities. Charles M. Blow makes this precise argument in the *New York Times* even as he misidentifies Precious's mother in the movie as a crack-addicted mother. (The *Times* noted the error on the website soon after the article appeared in print.) The oversight is crucial, considering that the main point of Blow's op-ed piece was to highlight the stark disparities between representations of black drug use on the big screen versus in society. The fact that Blow fails to see the uniqueness of Precious's mother's social circumstances and lumps her into what he calls the "crack-baby myth" made popular by President Ronald Reagan shines light on his limited vision of black women and class struggles as much as it does on the whites and opportunistic blacks he accuses, such as Tyler Perry, for cashing in on black stereotypes.[17] Even Melissa Harris-Perry (no relation to Tyler), a black feminist and staunch proponent of black women's rights, becomes guilty of a similar class and caste preoccupation with white perspectives of the black poor. Though Harris-Perry does not mis-identify Precious's mother as a crack addict, she asserts – like Blow – that the mother character reinforces portraits of such depictions of poor black mothering. Drawing a link between the popularity of the movie and the media obsession with Shaniya Davis (a five-year-old girl who was pimped out by her drug-addicted mother and found dead along a North Carolina roadside), Harris-Perry argues that the depiction of poor black mothering in *Precious* sends the wrong message to whites: "In a country with tens of thousands of missing and exploited children, it is not accidental that the abuse and murder of Shaniya Davis captured the American media cycle just as *Precious* opened. The sickening acts of Shaniya's mother became the story that underlines and makes tan-gible, believable, and credible the jaw-dropping horror of Mo'Nique's character."[18]

Based upon Harris-Perry's logic here, *Precious* – and movies like it that highlight unflattering portraits of blacks – give credence to the dangerous stereotypes about black women and mothering. As history demonstrates, however, stereotypes about black inferiority were, and are, necessary components to white domination in our society. That is, stereotyping black folks as inherently pathological and displacing blame for slavery and white oppression onto them are longstanding strategies of white domination. To suggest that black folks need to avoid making movies that depict us in ways that accommodate these strategies of white dominance is to ignore the glaring reality that the racial identity game, so to speak, is always already rigged. Even if the Preciouses of the world didn't exist – and they absolutely do – white institutions of power would invent them, just as they invented the idea of the "benevolent master" during slavery. Now, as it was then, manipulating black realities to re-flect white desires and motives rules the day. The fact that the movie *The Blind Side* – based on the "true" story of a petite, beautiful, gun-toting right winger coming to the rescue of a gigantic, strong, but sexually non-threatening black boy – was a runaway hit, outpacing the sales of *Precious* many times over and securing Sandra Bullock, the lead actress, an Oscar is a rather striking case in point. The overarching racial message of this "feel-good" movie is that individual acts of kindness by whites toward blacks, at bottom, trump this country's long and sordid history of racism and structural inequalities.

By prioritizing what white people think in this intraracial debate over *Precious,* opponents of the movie back themselves into a troubling political corner as it concerns the socioeconomic realities of the black poor. Intent notwithstanding, the political thrust of such a position reinforces the idea that whites are unaware, if not completely oblivious, to how they have dehumanized and disenfranchised blacks over time. In seeking on one level to debunk black stereotypes in the eyes of whites and offer "corrective" representations and prescriptions, this group (reflecting many of the class biases and blind spots of their talented-tenth forebears) overshoots the mark, denying our community failings and, by extension, the tragic toll that sustained white oppression and disenfranchisement has wreaked on generations of black minds and bodies. It is one thing to say that the depiction of black reality in *Precious* is representative of only a minority of black folks, and quite another to argue that the representations in the movie are not, as Harris-Perry asserts, "believable" or "tangible" at all.[19] Harris-Perry, in fact, gives an account of just such a reality in the Shaniya Davis case before beckoning her reader to reject as "truth" Mo'nique's riveting portrait of bad mothering in *Precious.* The contradiction is hardly subtle.

In *Lose Your Mother,* Saidiya Hartman explains the problems of black appeals to whites for fair and humane treatments. Hartman invokes Josiah Wedgwood's famous antislavery medallion depicting a kneeling slave begging for his humanity, with a banner underneath his figure reading, "Am I not a man and a brother?" She rightly argues that the racial calculus in the United States, beginning with slavery, that has compelled blacks into this position of relying on their captors and enslavers to confirm their humanity renders that strategy ultimately counterproductive: "Needing to make the case that we have suffered and that slavery, segregation, and racism have had a devastating effect on black life is the contemporary analogue to the defeated posture of Wedgwood's pet Negro. The apologetic density of the plea for recognition is staggering. It assumes both the ignorance and the innocence of the white world. If only they knew the truth, they would act otherwise."[20]

"Good" white folks in this case – meaning whites that feel guilty and become "excited" to sympathy at the spectacle of black suffering – get to have their racial sympathy cake and eat it too. That is, by "agitating" against slavery and for recognizing black suffering, they are handsomely rewarded socially by undying black gratitude. Though they constitute the direct cause of black dehumanization, they get to play the savior and martyr for black causes, a posture that strengthens rather than breaks the paternalistic black/white power relationship. Escaped slave Harriet Jacobs's predicament in *Incidents in the Life of a Slave Girl* puts a finer point on the issue. On the run in the North from her Southern enslavers, she explicitly tells her paternalistic white employer – who offers to buy Jacobs's freedom and end her fugitive status – that she would rather remain on the run than submit to the idea of being someone else's property. Yet, while Jacobs is in hiding, the white mistress buys her freedom anyway. Then afterwards and with paternalistic zeal, she expects Jacobs to be relieved and grateful. Though a shocked and disheartened Jacobs pays the obligatory dues to her white benefactress and new slave-owner (which is her legal status no matter how her benefactress romanticizes it), the reader recognizes that the white mistress never fully sees Jacobs or acknowledges her humanity. It is hardly a stretch to say that had Jacobs expressed indignation at her white mistress's insensitivity, she – not her white mistress – would have emerged in the public eye as the shortsighted and ungrateful one.

The twenty-first-century version of paternalistic, liberal whites are, at least partly, the audience Harris-Perry, Blow, Reed, and White have in mind when they blast the representation of black poverty and sexual abuse in *Precious*. White folks will think this representation is real, the thinking goes, because the movie is written, directed, acted, and, partly bankrolled, by *us*. The faulty racial logic upon which this thinking is based – that whites do not possess the mental capacity to recognize the social, economic, and cultural diversity within black communities and that they prioritize the hard facts of black realities over invented social fictions of black inferiority – places the modern-day talented tenth in the familiar position of educating a presumed ignorant and innocent white populace; a white populace, by the way, that has more at stake politically, socially, and economically in maintaining the status quo than in upsetting it. The aforementioned media love fest over *The Blind Side* and more recently *The Help* is but one of a slew of examples of the currency that such distorted depictions of racial realties and self-determination still have among whites.

Conspicuously missing from many of these attacks against *Precious* is also an acknowledgement of the shame- and inferiority complex–inducing effects of sustained white supremacy. As a child growing up in the South during the 1970s and 1980s, I remember acutely the venom that blacks directed at each other on the basis of their Afrocentric appearance. Among my most painful childhood memories is that of being mercilessly teased by my black peers for having a "pig nose" and "nappy hair," and being "black as an African." As stated in chapter 5, the idea of "good" and "bad" hair and the communal directive to stay out of the sun to avoid turning too black were so commonplace in my environment that I never gave them a moment's thought until I got to college and began studying – mostly on my own and *outside* the classroom – African American history and culture. Being poor – as many of my peers and close relatives were – only compounded the peer harassment; the only exceptions extended to those with stand-out athletic abilities, physical attraction, or some desirable social skill, like being a good rapper, singer, artist, or dancer. Suffice it to say that it would have been open season in my environment on someone of the gender, hue, class status, and size of the character Precious.

As one of the handful of blacks on the academically gifted track at the mostly white public high school I attended, I confronted the direct source of this self-hate in the classroom, where I was more often than not the lone black person in the class and where racist jokes and comments from students and teachers alike flowed freely. (I was once told by a white teacher, who was surprised by my emotional response to an uttered racial slur in the class, that when she was a teenager her peer group referred to blacks as "niggers" all the time and it was "no big deal.") Pressed into the posture of having always to speak on behalf of, and most often in defense of, "the race," I became hypersensitive to exploding white expectations of black inferiority. So much so, in fact, that at the time I often recoiled in anger at black folks that I viewed as reinforcing stereotypes and casting a negative light on "the race."

Looking back, I recognize that my schizophrenic racial predicament was not mere happenstance. In an environment where whiteness is
synonymous with normalcy, where it encapsulates all that is redeeming
about our culture, and where it is pitted diametrically against blackness as a marker of lack and primitivism, my reactions were certainly
understandable, if not also predictable. As the much-hyped book *Nurture Shock: New Thinking about Children* brought to public attention
(although the book merely cites research that has been available for
some time), the learned behavior of racism, and of racial inferiority for
black children, begins before toddlers can even utter full sentences.
The book presents an illustrative experiment: a racially mixed kindergarten class is introduced to the idea of a black Santa Claus, and the
children – black and white in this instance – go haywire. The gist of the
study is as follows. During the Christmas holiday season, two racially
diverse first grade classes were read *Twas the Night B'fore Christmas*
(1996), Melodye Rosales's Afrocentric recasting of Clement C. Moore's
classic Eurocentric tale, to test their racial reactions. After hearing the
Afrocentric version, complete with an African American Santa Claus,
the children began to discuss the racial components of the story without any prompting. Most of the white children rejected the idea out
of hand, though several modified their views slightly throughout the
week-long experiment, allowing for the ideas that black Santa might
be white Santa's helper or cousin. The experiment culminated in the
actual appearance of a black Santa at the end of the week. As might be
expected, the physical appearance of black Santa amplified the racial
discussion. Bronson and Merryman report that the black children were
"exultant" about black Santa Claus's arrival, because it "proved [presum-
ably to the white kids as much as to themselves] that Santa was black."[21]
Faced with the material reality of a black Santa, the white children were
thrown into a bit of a crisis. A few handled the crisis by trying directly to
"discredit" black Santa, calling attention to his "thin" frame or invoking
encounters with the "real" white Santa in other venues such as K-Mart.
The overwhelming majority of them, however, resolved this crisis not
by abandoning the white Santa idea, but by intensifying their effort to
fit the black Santa into the dominant narrative as a "sidekick" or special
helper of some kind.

What struck a personal emotional chord with me as a father was the authors' depiction of Brent, a rather outspoken black boy in the classroom who is around my daughter Octavia's age. Whereas most of the children are rather passive in the presence of black Santa Claus, Brent confronts him openly and aggressively, remarking "There ain't no black Santas!"[22] When the black Santa asks Brent, "What color do you see?" Brent responds incredulously, "Black – but under your socks you might not be!"[23] Only after black Santa pulls up his pant leg, revealing black ankles, does Brent finally believe. He bellows enthusiastically, "This is a black Santa! . . . He's got black skin and his black boots are like the white Santa's boots!"[24] After chronicling Brent's celebration, the authors tell us that despite black Santa's visit to class, *all* the children depicted Santa as "snowy-white" when later they were asked to draw a portrait of him on paper.

Paule Marshall registers a similar level of contaminated racial consciousness in *Praisesong for a Widow*, when the child protagonist Avey openly questions her Aunt Cuney's account of a band of African Ibos brought over on a slave ship who decided, after surveying their circumstances and seeing into the future of slavery, to walk back to Africa over the Atlantic Ocean. When Avey – who has heard the story told many times since her birth – asks her aunt incredulously how the Ibos kept from drowning, her aunt fires back indignantly, "Did it [the Bible] say Jesus drowned when he went walking on the water in . . . [your] Sunday School book . . . ?" Avey, responds, "No, ma'am." Aunt Cuney then follows up, "I din' think so. You got any more questions?" Embarrassed and outdone, Avey responds, "No."[25] In the conversation, Aunt Cuney exposes her niece's white male supremacist indoctrination, which prompts her to embrace as plausible the biblical account of a white Jesus walking on water but to dismiss out of hand a story that involves Africans doing the exact same thing.

Given the lasting scars that being immersed in such a toxic racial environment can leave on one's mind, body, and soul, it comes as no surprise that a movie like *Precious* has elicited such an intense and passionate response from the black middle class. As Nicholas Powers poignantly asserts, the representation of pain, hurt, and agony are color-coded and camouflaged in our society in such a way as to displace white moral, social, and political crises onto blacks. This racial equation gives rise to "black damage imagery" as a bankable commodity;[26] a commodity that helps sell everything from hip hop to the death penalty. The proliferation of this commodity and "so many monstrous reflections of ourselves" drives many black folks to buy into propaganda and, concomitantly, black middle class gatekeepers to engage in "Uncle Tom" witch hunts.[27] Recalling Hughes's call to political arms in "The Negro Artist and the Racial Mountain," Powers tries to reconfigure the race and class terms of the debate. He writes that when critics accuse Sapphire and the movie *Precious* of "using black damage imagery that gives whites the pleasure of voyeurism . . . [and] displacing [white] anxiety" onto blacks, "we should turn the dialectical wheel." He then expounds, "Should victims of systemic oppression not show symptoms of it? Is black on black crime not one of them? Is it not true that the powerless often attack those weaker than they? Why can't we say that this happens with us too? Men attack women. Mothers attack children. Memories attack the present. How can we heal if we can't see how we hurt each other?"[28]

What Powers brings radically into focus is the political slippage of allowing whites not only to dictate the terms of black pain, but also to dictate the terms of black recovery and healing. Though fending off white claims of black pathology is important and necessary, it trivializes rather than ameliorates the suffering of black folks to deny the scars – physical, emotional, and spiritual – that we bear from systemic white domination. Powers articulates this dangerous racial trap brilliantly in the comment section of his blog when he comes under fire from the aforementioned Ishmael Reed for perpetuating white supremacy: "When we can't admit that institutional racism has misshapen us, we condemn ourselves to a stoic silence that saps our strength instead of freeing it. So instead of repeating ad nauseam one reading of *Precious*, that it's a tool of white supremacy, try acknowledging the painful experiences it shows are also a product of it. Many women need to have their pain acknowledged without being made to feel guilty for betraying the race."[29]

Powers's comments demonstrate the razor-thin line between challenging the white supremacist status quo and accommodating it. The point is not to produce a new rubric to determine who is selling out, but to acknowledge openly and honestly the slipperiness of the political enterprise in which we all have deep intellectual, political, and emotional stakes. Indeed, the cold hard fact is that the very group under scrutiny in this *Precious* debate – poor black folks – remain invisible in their myriad complexity to the country at large. And, with few exceptions, the voice and opinions of this population have also been largely ignored, even at the level of intraracial discussions. Made clear by, say, Katie Couric's exclusive interview with Sapphire, and the ways various dominant media outlets treated the *Precious* debate, is the fact that middle-class blacks operate as the unofficial stand-in for all of black America. Though this pattern has been in place for some time, it encourages many of us – including those sensitive to the extent to which class/status shapes the experience of "race," racism, and gender – to speak as the voice of the black poor rather than as the class- and education-advantaged group that we are. And, yes, this also includes folks who, like me, have moved up a rung or two on the socioeconomic ladder from the status of their birth. That such introspection on the level of class has been largely absent from public debate, both in and beyond black circles, reveals precisely why we must always be mindful of our potential blind spots when engaging so-called black realities. An inevitability of being a socially marginalized group is that we are highly vulnerable to having our words, arts, politics, religion, and scholarship misinterpreted or even outright hijacked to support politically anti-black agendas. (It was, in fact, because of this potentiality, and her heightened sensitivity to black girls' suffering, that Sapphire turned down multiple, lucrative deals before agreeing to let Lee Daniels – whom she also rejected multiple times – make the movie.) Well within our control, however, are the terms upon which we choose to address each other and the obstacles – imposed and self-generated – that plague our various communities. The *Precious* debate has, among other things, exposed the extent to which we have yet, as a group, to develop a productive way to contend with intraracial class issues. Though it is impossible to determine when, or whether, this issue can be productively resolved, one thing is for sure. The Preciouses of the world – real and imagined – are not going away any time soon.

Come out of the fog, young man. And remember you don't have to be a complete fool in order to succeed. Play the game, but don't believe in it – that much you owe yourself. Even if it lands you in a strait jacket or a padded cell. Play the game, but play it your way – part of the time at least. Play the game, but raise the ante, my boy. Learn how it operates, learn how *you* operate – I wish I had time to tell you only a fragment. We're an ass-backward people, though. You might even beat the game. It's really a very crude affair. Really pre-Renaissance – and that game has been analyzed, put down in books. But down here they've forgotten to take care of the books and that's your opportunity. *You're hidden right out in the open* – that is, you would be if you only realized it. They wouldn't see you because they don't expect you to know anything, since they believe they've taken care of that . . .

Ralph Ellison, *Invisible Man*

Epilogue: So What Does It All Mean?

THE EPIGRAPH FROM RALPH ELLISON'S *INVISIBLE MAN* IS THE advice that the "crazy" vet from the Golden Day – a bar/juke joint where a bunch of "shell-shocked" black war veterans hang out – gives invisible man as he heads north to find an internship after being expelled from his university for mishandling Mr. Norton, a millionaire white philanthropist. As the reader will recall, invisible man first encounters the crazy vet at the Golden Day. After Mr. Norton passes out during the melee at the bar, sparked in large part by his white presence, the vet and former surgeon revives him and rightly diagnoses the medical cause of his unconsciousness. When Mr. Norton inquires about his medical knowledge, the vet tells him about his experiences in the military as a brain surgeon; how acts of dehumanization and violence led to ulcers and his becoming sour on the notion that black accommodationism is the most viable path to success and prosperity in America: "These hands so lovingly trained to master a scalpel yearn to caress a trigger. I returned to save life and I was refused. . . . Ten [white] men in masks drove me out from the city at midnight and beat me with whips for saving a human life. And I was forced to the utmost degradation because I possessed skilled hands and the belief that my knowledge could bring me dignity – and other men health!"[1] While the vet does not provide Mr. Norton or the reader with details about the particulars of his racial beat down, we can deduce that he was brutally beaten because he operated on a white person, and most likely a white woman, in a life-or-death scenario and was rewarded for his heroics with violence and humiliation. Though the virulently paternalistic and blind Mr. Norton labels him bitter, the reality is that the vet is justifiably indignant – he tried to use his surgical skills to save white lives even though, as a group, whites were chiefly responsible for his socioeconomic subjugation as a black man. In effect, he played by the white supremacist rules of black accommodationism and still couldn't avoid racial violence and dehumanization.

When the vet registers that invisible man is too infatuated with whiteness and blind ambition to appreciate his cautionary tale, he explains to Mr. Norton, as invisible man listens in, that such blind black faith in white goodwill is tragic and dangerous: "Already he is . . . a walking zombie! Already he's learned to repress not only his emotions but his humanity. He's invisible, a walking personification of the Negative, the most perfect achievement of your [Mr. Norton's] dreams, sir! The mechanical man!"[2] He goes on to say that to Mr. Norton, invisible man is not a person but a "mark on the scorecard of your achievement, a thing and not a man; a child, or even less – a black amorphous thing." He tells Mr. Norton that invisible man sees him "not [as] a man . . . but a God, a force [of nature]."[3] The vet then angrily lectures them both as Mr. Norton, who is deeply offended, attempts to leave: "He believes in you as he believes in the beat of his heart. He believes in that great false wisdom taught slaves and pragmatists alike, that white is right. I can tell you *his* destiny. He'll do your bidding, and for that his blindness is his chief asset. He's your man, friend. Your man and your destiny." Despite himself, invisible man is intrigued, if not impressed, by the vet's fearlessness. "The vet was acting toward the white man with a freedom which could only bring on trouble. I wanted to tell Mr. Norton that the man was crazy and yet I received a fearful satisfaction from hearing him talk as he had to a white man."[4] What is indeed empowering about the vet's actions and words is that he is fearless to the point of death. He sees Mr. Norton as the paternalist, self-congratulatory racial parasite that he is, rather than the benevolent, omniscient God-force that invisible man and the black elites at the college believe him to be. The vet is dangerous politically to this extent, not only because he has nothing to lose in being brutally honest (he's already been dehumanized, violently assaulted, and run out of the medical profession), but also because he prioritizes truth-telling over life. Mr. Norton's power as a white man to control and dominate him are thus radically neutralized, for the goal of white supremacist power is not to destroy black bodies (genocide was never seriously in the cards) but to render them subordinate to white ones, and specifically those of the white elite. This may, in fact, explain why, instead of physically harming the vet, Mr. Norton allegedly fast-tracks the vet's request to be transferred to a psychological facility in Washington, D.C.: "I can't but wonder," says the vet to invisible man at the train station, "if our little conversation with your friend Mr. Norton had something to do with it."

The wicked paradox here, of course, is that however bold and revolutionary are the vet's deconstruction of white supremacist power and blacks' unconscious and conscious complicity in it, he is ultimately a non-threat because in the public domain, and in black spaces, his radicalism is misread as insanity. Metaphorically speaking, he is a general without an army; a coach without a team; a teacher without students. Mr. Norton – the embodiment of white male power – is not taking any chances, though. The act of shipping him off to Washington and away from the white-controlled and -funded black college is an offensive move. This is clearly an unthought known gesture on Mr. Norton's part. He knows, even if he refuses to see, that the vet's insights have the potential of exploding the myth of white supremacy and thus compromising his and whites' chief means of ideological domination over black communities. In a word, Mr. Norton knows the vet ain't crazy, even if he has plenty of political and economic reasons to act as if he is. Leaving him in such close proximity to smart, ambitious young black minds at the college is obviously a risk he is not willing to take.

But let's be clear. The advice that the vet gives invisible man at the train station is not exactly clear. How does one participate in "the game" of white power, even subversively, without being contaminated and/or compromised ideologically by it? Concomitantly, what does true subversion to white power look like? Moreover, what is the endgame of subversion? Will toppling white power from the bottom up lead to black empowerment or, better yet, racial equality?

That said, what is dangerous about the vet is not his confounding prescription for toppling white power or his advocacy of subversive action. Rather, it is his acute awareness that white supremacy is an invention that needs a black buy-in, in the form of complicity, in order to remain effective. The vet needn't have the exact formula for exploding white supremacy, then. He is a threat to dominant power by the simple fact that he has deciphered the code of white power; that he sees white supremacy as an ideology of empire rather than as organic to the human race; that he sees blackness as an imposed identity revealing nothing about his and African Americans' intellect, morality, and humanity in general.

It is hardly a coincidence that many of the black writers and thinkers under examination in *Blinded by the Whites* render their progressive racial politics through outcast figures. If the chief power of white supremacist ideology is to dictate what counts as reality – whether the issue at hand is racial experience, history, politics, violence, gender, sexuality, or nationhood – then the challenge before blacks and people of color is to defy this reality-making apparatus of power; to legitimize the illegitimate, make the invisible visible and speak the unspeakable. Toni Morrison puts it best in *Playing in the Dark: Whiteness and the Literary Imagination* when she avers that the "test" of a writer's power is her ability "to imagine what is not the self, to familiarize the strange and mystify the familiar."[5] While Morrison's framework is applicable to all writers across race lines, she is thinking here more specifically about black writers and writers of color on the margins, because theirs, as members of a raced and othered people, is a more daunting ideological task. If blacks and people of color are conditioned to be "personifications of the Negative," to borrow the vet's apt terminology, then affirming their complex humanity and personhood is itself a revolutionary act, one that requires fighting off the racial commonsense that "white is right," to invoke the vet again, and black, by default, is wrong.

What we know about the intersectionality of power – to borrow Kimberlé Crenshaw's black feminist framework[6] – is that the challenge before blacks and people of color is greater still as white supremacist ideology divides and conquers by getting marginalized folks to collude with it; to defend our provisional privileges from the margins as men who are black, women who are white, people who are straight, Christian, educated, and middle class. As I have hoped to bring into clearer focus in *Blinded by the Whites,* marginalized folks, especially those of us who have greater visibility and wield legitimate power, ignore these issues of complicity in oppression at our own peril. As the vet in *Invisible Man* makes clear, accommodating status quo power and then, by turns, reaping the meager economic and social spoils of being a "good negro" or model minority, is but another form of complicity in oppression. It should go without saying that dominant power – including major media outlets, the federal government, and, yes, the White House with the black president – will continue to vilify those of us who dare reject the egalitarian propaganda that we live in a post-oppression society; still, history teaches us that ostracism, assault, and even death are, as James Baldwin would say, the "price of the ticket" to black empowerment and racial equality.

The crucial question before us, then, especially those of us on the outside looking in with regard to dominant economic and political power, is: Are we willing to make the necessary sacrifices (bodily, materially, and emotionally) to create the truly democratic society that we say we want? Only time will tell if we are willing to take on this challenge and follow the lead of those – handful that they were – who have put it on the line for black empowerment and human rights writ large. One thing is certain, however. If we accommodate the status quo – play by the rules of racial power imposed upon us rather than seeking to rewrite them – then we can expect more of the same in terms of racial hostility, dispropor-tionately high unemployment in black spaces, the rerouting of federal resources away from our communities, the ideological assaults on our children, and the like. What our struggles, from helping to abolish slav-ery to fighting for civil rights, have taught us is that the might, courage, brilliance, and determination of a few can be transformative in revolu-tionary ways. Likewise, we have learned from our failures on this score that nothing can kill a movement quicker than fear, complacency, and low expectations. Our destiny remains in our hands. If we want to alter it for the better, then political inaction and blind accommodationism are not viable options.[7] As one of my mentors of was fond of saying, "This ain't rocket science." The answers are hidden in plain sight.

Notes

INTRODUCTION

1. Ellison, *Invisible Man*, 4.
2. Ibid., 568.
3. Douglass, *The Narrative of the Life of Frederick Douglass*, 20.
4. Ibid.
5. Douglass makes a clear distinction between this type of unconscious black complicity, for which slaves should not be held accountable, and conscious black complicity (i.e., a willful desire to exploit black suffering for material or social gain), which he treats as reprehensible and deserving of death.
6. Ibid, 89.
7. Wise, *Between Barack and a Hard Place*, 33.
8. Ibid, 29.
9. Roediger is riffing on Malcolm X's comparison of white supremacy to the Cadillac car brand, the gist of Malcolm X's argument – as relayed via Roediger – being that white supremacy resembles the prestigious Cadillac brand, in that it shifts its model offerings (i.e., outward appearances) from year to year "but leave[s] the essence of the brand intact" (xiii). Roediger, *How Race Survived U.S. History*, xiii.
10. See Ikard and Teasley, *Nation of Cowards*.
11. Beatty, *The White Boy Shuffle*, 30.
12. Ibid.
13. Ibid., 31–32.
14. Mercer, *Welcome to the Jungle*, 103.
15. Eagleton, *The Significance of Theory*, 37.
16. Morrison, *Beloved*, 198.
17. George Zimmerman is of mixed raced heritage – one of his parents is white, the other Hispanic. I use "white" here to denote how Zimmerman self-identifies and is received in the public domain.
18. Cosby made these claims as the keynote speaker at the NAACP's banquet celebrating the fiftieth anniversary commemoration of the Brown v. Topeka Board of Education Supreme Court decision.
19. See Obama, *The Audacity of Hope*.
20. "The Negro Family: The Case for National Action," United States Department of Labor.
21. Mutua, *Progressive Black Masculinities*, 5.
22. Lorde, *Sister Outsider*, 40.
23. Hall, "Cultural Studies and Its Theoretical Legacies," in the *Norton Anthology of Theory and Criticism*, 1907.
24. Ibid., 1901.

1. WHITE SUPREMACY UNDER FIRE

1. Jones, *The Known World*, 153.
2. Ibid., 162.
3. Ibid., 163.

4. Donaldson, "Telling Forgotten Stories of Slavery in the Postmodern South," 271.

5. White indentured servants doubled in the colonies as a military force against Native American "insurgencies." Outnumbering the aristocracy by a significant margin, they were as a practical matter a force to be recognized with. It was then in the aristocracy's best social interest to build bridges with these groups – a reality that was made devastatingly clear in Bacon's Rebellion, when European and African indentured servants formed a coalition on the basis of shared oppression, took up arms, and tried to overthrow the power structure. While Jones does not directly engage this history in the novel, its presence looms large over how whites, especially the white poor, negotiate their social value in relation to blacks.

6. Dyer, *White*, 19.

7. In the ur-text of this political tradition, *Narrative of the Life of Frederick Douglass,* Douglass conveys white supremacist ideology as a contagion of pathology via Mrs. Auld – who after becoming a slave owner and being injected with "the fatal poison of irresponsible power" (35) moves from being the embodiment of moral virtue and "Christian" piety to becoming a cruel and heartless "demon." Identifying white supremacist ideology as an equal opportunity contaminant of humanity, Douglass concludes, "Slavery proved as injurious to her as it did to me" (39).

8. Donaldson, 271.

9. In his essay "Cultural Trauma: Slavery and the Formation of African American Identity," Eyerman describes "intellectuals" as mediators and translators of collective cultural memory and consciousness. These intellectuals are crucial to their representative groups because they "mediate between the cultural and political spheres that characterize modern society." When groups experience "tear[s]

in the social fabric" of their communities – like the realization by African Americans during the post-Reconstruction era that they were not going to be issued full citizenship as promised – intellectuals help them reinterpret "the past as a means toward reconciling present/future needs" (63).

10. Jones, "We Tell Stories."

11. Ibid.

12. Ibid.

13. This pattern has not escaped the attention of African American communities in the contemporary moment, as evidenced by filmmaker Spike Lee's *Bamboozled*, political cartoonist Aaron McGrudger's *Boondocks* animated series, and Dave Chappelle's *The Dave Chappelle Show.*

14. See Saidiya Hartman's *Lose Your Mother* for an insightful historical critique of African slavery and its similarities to and distinctions from European practices.

15. Addressing the accusation, in an interview with Maryemma Graham, that his novel lets whites off the hook for slavery, Jones asserts that many of his harshest critics on this score have not actually read the book. Citing a rather striking example of this phenomenon, he recalls how an African American man who had yet to read to the book called in to a radio program on which Jones was being interviewed, lambasting the novel as dangerous and Jones as irresponsible for writing it. After reading the text, however, he radically shifted his perspective, later approaching Jones in person at a public event and issuing an apology.

16. Baldwin, *The Fire Next Time*, 101.

17. Ibid., 95.

18. Morrison, *Playing in the Dark*, 57.

19. Ibid., 56.

20. Ibid.

21. Ibid., 56–57, my emphasis.

22. Ibid., 57.

23. Baldwin, *Fire*, 102.

24. Morrison, *Playing*, 17.

25. Yeager, *Dirt and Desire*, 103.

26. Jones, *Known World*, 151.

27. Carby, *Reconstructing Womanhood*, 55.

28. Jones, *Known World*, 76.

29. Newitz and Wray, "What Is 'White Trash?' Stereotypes and Economic Conditions of Poor Whites in the United States," 170.

30. Jones, *Known World* 42, my emphasis.

31. Ibid., 303, my emphasis.

32. Du Bois, "My Evolving Program," 70.

33. Jones, *Known World*, 37.

34. Ibid.

35. Ibid., 38.

36. Ibid.

37. Ibid., 40.

38. Ibid., 21.

39. Ibid., 120.

40. Ibid., 348.

41. Ibid., 382.

42. Ibid., 381.

43. Ibid.

44. Ibid., 348.

45. Ibid.

46. Ibid., 375.

47. Ibid., 94.

48. Ibid., 64, italics in text.

49. Ibid., 123.

50. Ibid., 300.

51. Ibid., 253.

52. Morrison, *Beloved*, 109.

53. Jones, *Known World*, 375.

54. Ibid., 198.

55. Ibid., 130.

56. Ibid., 286.

57. In "Imagining Other Worlds: Race, Gender, and the 'Power Line,'" Bassard usefully historicizes this phenomenon of gifting freedom, which always already positions the master as the true philanthropist even in cases where slaves, like Augustus, have to purchase their freedom.

58. Ibid., 260.

59. Ibid.

60. Caldonia's brother Calvin also undergoes a transformation and ends up denouncing slavery outright.

61. Morrison, *Beloved*, 316.

2. EASIER SAID THAN DONE

1. Morrison, *Beloved*, 231.

2. Ibid., 273.

3. As a writer, Morrison intentionally leaves out key information in her texts to press the reader to become conscious of the racialized act of reading and meaning making. This strategy is most obvious in her short story "Recitatif" and her novel *Paradise*. Consequently, in *Beloved* she also conspicuously withholds the race of the white man that Sethe has sex with to pay for the tombstone of the child that she kills.

4. Morrison, *Beloved*, 273.

5. Ibid.

6. As Dwight McBride, Michael Awkward, and Eric Pritchard have rightly argued, gay black men also possess and traffic in intraracial male privilege. I focus on black heternormative men here, then, not because they are the only black male group that exploits male privilege, but because they are, without a doubt, the group most resistant to black feminism.

7. Though is it certainly important to give credit where credit is due, so to speak, I would argue that it is far more important that black men embrace the concepts of black feminism than it is that they associate themselves with the movement or political brand.

8. Awkward quoting Spillers's "Mama's Baby, Papa's Maybe."

9. Awkward, "A Black Man's Place in Black Feminist Criticism."

10. Ibid., 54.

11. Ibid., 53.

12. Ibid., 54.

13. In her iconic essay, "In Search of Our Mothers' Gardens," Walker repur-

poses the term "womanish" – an epithet black men use to castigate outspoken and rebellious women – to describe a redeeming impulse by black women to fight back against black patriarchy. Concomitantly, Walker coined the term "womanist" to describe black women who openly embraced this defiant, feminist attitude.

14. From my mother's perspective, she was the true victim. Some years later, after I pressed my mother to explain her rationale, she explained that she had been a victim of attempted sexual assault at the hands of family members but had managed to fight them off. To her mind, if my aunt truly did not want to have sex with my father she would have fought him off as well. My mother forgave my father because she saw it as her Christian duty as a wife.

15. Soon after my "epiphany" I began writing letters to my aunt to voice my support and understanding of her situation. I wrote a total of five or six letters. Though she never wrote back, my othered sister let me know that my aunt had received and read the letters.

16. Hill Collins, "A Telling Difference: Dominance, Strength, and Black Masculinities," 73.

17. This phenomenon is encapsulated in *Their Eyes* as well when the lower-class men recast Jody – the most powerful and revered man in town – as weak for "allowing" Janie to insult his masculinity in public.

18. Ibid., 75.
19. Ibid.
20. Ibid.
21. Neal, *New Black Man*, 71.
22. Mutua, *Progressive Black Masculinities*, 18.
23. Morrison, *Beloved*, 274.
24. Ibid., 276.
25. Ibid., 277. (My italics)
26. Ibid., 321.

3. ALL JOKING ASIDE

1. Beatty, *The White Boy Shuffle*, 131.
2. Ibid., 131.
3. Ibid., 131.
4. Pyun, "Review of *The White Boy Shuffle*, by Paul Beatty."
5. Haggins, *Laughing Mad.*
6. Michelle Obama, interview with Steve Kroft.
7. Dickson-Carr, *African American Satire*, 168.
8. Ibid., p. 205.
9. Beatty, *White Boy Shuffle*, 96.
10. Ibid., 96.
11. Stallings, "Punked For Life," 110.
12. Hill Collins, "A Telling Difference," 75.
13. Ibid., 75.
14. Beatty, *White Boy Shuffle*, 34.
15. Ibid., 35.
16. Ibid., 36.
17. Ibid., 36.
18. Ibid., 9.
19. Ibid., 9.
20. Ibid., 10.
21. Ibid., 10.
22. Ibid., 12.
23. Ibid., 21.
24. Ibid., 21.
25. Mutua, "Theorizing Progressive Black Masculinities."
26. Beatty, *White Boy Shuffle*, 53.
27. Ibid., 47.
28. Ibid., 47.
29. Ibid., 51.
30. Ibid., 144.
31. Ibid., 138. My emphasis.
32. Ibid., 138.
33. *Bigger and Blacker,* DVD.
34. Beatty, *White Boy Shuffle*, 138.
35. Murray, "Black Crisis Shuffle: Fiction, Race, and Simulation," 230.
36. Beatty, *White Boy Shuffle*, 147.
37. See Cathy J. Cohen's essay "Punks, Bulldaggers, and Welfare Queens: The Radical Potential of Queer Politics?"

38. Ibid., 148.

39. Morrison, *Playing in the Dark: Whiteness and the Literary Imagination*, 15.

40. Beatty, *White Boy Shuffle*, 226.

41. Ibid., 226.

4. BOYS TO MEN

1. Soulja Boy, "The DeAndre Way," 2010.

2. Ibid.

3. Jack Mirkinson, "CNN Suspends Roland Martin For 'Offensive' Super Bowl Tweets," *Huffington Post*.

4. Mercer, *Welcome to the Jungle*, 137.

5. Ibid.

6. Ibid.

7. Blow, "Real Men and Pink Suits."

8. See Maia Szalavitz's "Study: Whites More Likely to Abuse Drugs Than Blacks."

9. Wise, *Between Barack and a Hard Place*, 23.

10. Neal, *New Black Man*, 24.

11. Ibid.

12. Ibid.

13. Ibid., 30.

14. McBride, *Why I Hate Abercrombie and Fitch*, 92.

15. Ibid.

16. Ibid

17. Audre Lorde quoted in McBride, *Why I Hate Abercrombie and Fitch*, 93.

18. Beatty, *White Boy Shuffle*, 153.

5. REJECTING GOLDILOCKS

1. Ikard and Teasley, *Nation of Cowards*, co-authored with Martell Lee Teasley.

2. Norton and Sommers, "Whites See Racism as a Zero-Sum Game That They Are Now Losing," 215.

3. I am referring to the ways that white feminists and black male nationalists have historically used black women's suffering to make the case for their self-interested political agendas, not to empower black women.

4. Bonilla-Silva, "'New Racism,' Color-Blind Racism, and the Future of Whiteness in America," 271.

5. Baldwin, *The Fire Next Time*, 6.

6. I should add that Michelle Obama's favorability ratings among whites are at an all-time high, which I suspect has a lot to do with the fact that she has accommodated a more traditional gender posture while in the White House.

7. Mercer, *Welcome to the Jungle*; citation from 101.

8. Ibid., 100.

9. "Melissa Harris-Perry Show," MSNBC, June 10, 2012.

10. Byrd and Tharps, *Hair Story*, 41.

11. Hill Collins, *Black Sexual Politics*, 194.

12. Hurston, *Their Eyes Were Watching God*, 139.

13. See my essay "Ruthless Individuality and the Other(ed) Black Women in Zora Neale Hurston's *Their Eyes Were Watching God*."

14. Hurston, *Their Eyes*, 140–141.

15. Ibid., 141.

16. Ibid., 140.

17. Hurston, *Dust Tracks on a Road*, 189.

18. I should mention here that Hurston wrote *Dust Tracks* under tremendous financial pressure and with an unspoken publishing mandate to cater to a white readership, obstacles that Robert Hemenway, Deborah G. Plant, Nellie McKay and others have called attention to as a way to account for Hurston's conspicuous soft-pedaling on white culpability in black oppression.

19. Michael Awkward, Mary Helen Washington, and Nellie McKay are some of the most outspoken scholars on this score.

20. Wright, "Between Laughter and Tears," 23.

21. Schuyler, *Black No More*, 54.

22. Ellison, *Invisible Man*, 101.

23. I discuss this phenomenon in great detail in my book *Breaking the Silence*.

24. Morrison, *The Bluest Eye*, 65.

25. Ibid., 66–67.

26. Ibid., 74.

27. Nelly, "Tip Drill."

28. Mark Anthony Neal discusses this issue at length in *New Black Man*.

29. Sharpley-Whiting, *Pimps Up, Ho's Down: Hip Hop's Hold on Young Black Women*, 38.

30. "Santaluces High School in Florida on Alert after 2 Teens Post Racist Video."

31. Pitts, "Happy-To-Be-Nappy Barbie."

32. Ibid., Ann Ducille quoted in Pitts.

33. Ibid.

34. Jami, comment on Williams, "A Black Princess."

6. "STOP MAKING THE REST OF US LOOK BAD"

1. Ellison, "The World and the Jug," 130–131.

2. I mention that Tyson is white only to show how the white student is privileging race in determining critical authority. Tyson would certainly not have condoned how this student was (mis)appropriating his pedagogy.

3. Everett, *Erasure*, 261.

4. Ibid., 261, my emphasis.

5. Ibid., 262.

6. Ibid., 212.

7. Du Bois, "Criteria of Negro Art," 66.

8. Ibid., 64.

9. Washington, *Medical Apartheid* 197.

10. Johnson, *Autobiography of an Ex-Colored Man*, 77.

11. Hughes, "The Negro Artist and the Racial Mountain," 59.

12. White, "Pride and Precious."

13. Reed, "The Selling of Precious," online.

14. White, "Pride and Precious."

15. Reed, "The Selling of Precious."

16. Reed first posted in the comment section on Mark Anthony Neal's blog *New Black Man*, taking Neal to task for defending the movie and referencing Neal's affiliation with Duke University's women's studies program. Neal is a professor at Duke. Reed subsequently surfaced in the comment section on my blog, *Nation of Cowards*, in response to my post about his attack on black feminist supporters of the movie. He later emailed me directly, making the case that Lee Daniels was politically compromised because of his coziness with Hollywood and queer politics. His response to Power's blog post, which is quoted in this chapter, takes a similar political trajectory.

17. Blow, "Tyler Perry's Crack Mothers."

18. Harris-Perry, "Bad Black Mothers."

19. Ibid.

20. Hartman, *Lose Your Mother*, 169.

21. Bronson and Merryman, *Nurture Shock*, 68.

22. Ibid., 68.

23. Ibid., 68.

24. Ibid., 69.

25. Marshall, *Praisesong for a Widow*, 40.

26. Powers, "'Precious' or How I Learned to Stop Worrying and Love the Movie."

27. Ibid.

28. Ibid.

29. Ibid.

EPILOGUE

1. Ellison, *Invisible Man*, 93.

2. Ibid., 94.

3. Ibid., 95.

4. Ibid., 93.

5. Morrison, *Playing in the Dark*, 15.

NOTES TO PAGES 154–155

6. See "Mapping the Margins: Intersectionality, Identity Politics, and Violence against Women of Color."

7. When I say political here, I mean more than just voting or participating in the political process, all of which are necessary and important to empowerment; I also have in mind moving to action on issues, be they local, national, or international, that threaten human rights and social justice.

Bibliography

Awkward, Michael. "A Black Man's Place in Black Feminist Criticism." In *Negotiating Difference: Race, Gender, and the Politics of Positionality*. Chicago: University of Chicago Press, 1995.

Baldwin, James. *The Fire Next Time*. New York: Random House, 1993.

Bassard, Katherine Clay. "Imagining Other Worlds: Race, Gender, and the 'Power Line' in Edward P. Jones's *The Known World*." *African American Review* 42.3–4 (Fall/Winter 2008): 407–419.

Beatty, Paul. *The White Boy Shuffle*. New York: Picador, 1996.

Blow, Charles. "Real Men and Pink Suits." *New York Times*, February 2, 2012, http://www.nytimes.com/2012/02/11/opinion/blow-real-men-and-pink-suits.html.

———. "Tyler Perry's Crack Mothers." *New York Times*, February 26, 2010, http://www.nytimes.com/2010/02/27/opinion/27 blow.html.

Bonilla-Silva, Eduardo. "'New Racism,' Color-Blind Racism, and the Future of Whiteness in America." In *White Out: The Continuing Significance of Racism*, edited by Ashley W. Doane and Eduardo Bonilla-Silva. New York: Routledge, 2003.

Boyz n the Hood. Directed by John Singleton, 1991. Los Angeles: Sony Pictures Home Entertainment, 1998. DVD.

Bronson, Po, and Ashley Merryman. *Nurture Shock: New Thinking about Children*. New York: Twelve, 2009.

Carby, Hazel. *Reconstructing Womanhood: The Emergence of the Afro-American Woman Novelist*. Oxford: Oxford University Press, 1987.

Cleaver, Eldridge. *Soul on Ice*. New York: Random House, 1968.

Crenshaw, Kimberlé W. "Mapping the Margins: Intersectionality, Identity Politics, and Violence against Women of Color." *Stanford Law Review* 43.6 (1991):1241–1299.

Cohen, Cathy J. "Punks, Bulldaggers, and Welfare Queens: The Radical Potential of Queer Politics?" GLQ 3 (1997): 437–465.

Dickson-Carr, Darryl. *African American Satire: The Sacredly Profane Novel*. Columbia: University of Missouri Press, 2001.

Donaldson, Susan V. "Telling Forgotten Stories of Slavery in the Postmodern South." *Southern Literary Journal* 40.2 (Spring 2008): 267–283.

Douglass, Frederick. *The Narrative of the Life of Frederick Douglass, An American Slave*. New York: Barnes & Noble Classics, 2003.

Du Bois, W. E. B. "Criteria of Negro Art." In Angelyn Mitchell, ed., *Within the Circle*.

———. "My Evolving Program for Negro Freedom." In *What the Negro Wants,* edited by Rayford W. Logan. Chapel Hill: University of North Carolina Press, 1944.

Dyer, Richard. *White.* London: Routledge, 1997.

Eagleton, Terry, and Michael Payne. *The Significance of Theory.* Chichester, UK: Wiley-Blackwell, 1991.

Ellison, Ralph. *Invisible Man.* New York: Random House, 1995.

———. "The World and the Jug." In *Shadow and Act.* New York: Random House, 1995.

Everett, Percival. *Erasure.* Hanover: Graywolf Press, 2011.

Eyerman, Ron. "Cultural Trauma: Slavery and the Formation of African American Identity." In *Cultural Trauma and Collective Identity,* edited by Jeffery C. Alexander, Ron Eyerman, Bernard Giesen and Piotr Sztompka. Berkeley: University of California Press, 2004.

Good Hair. Directed by Jeff Stilson. Los Angeles: Lionsgate Home Entertainment, 2001. DVD.

Haggins, Bambi. *Laughing Mad: The Black Comic Persona in Post-Soul America.* New Brunswick: Rutgers University Press, 2007.

Hall, Stuart. "Cultural Studies and Its Theoretical Legacies." In *The Norton Anthology of Theory and Criticism,* edited by Vincent B. Leitch, William E. Cain, Laurie A. Finke, and Barbara E. Johnson] New York: W. W. Norton, 2001.

Harris-Perry, Melissa. "Bad Black Mothers." Review of the movie *Precious,* directed by Lee Daniels. *The Nation,* November 24, 2009, http://www.the-nation.com/blog/bad-black-mothers.

Hartman, Saidiya. *Lose Your Mother.* New York: Farrar, Straus, and Giroux, 2007.

Hill Collins, Patricia. "A Telling Difference: Dominance, Strength, and Black Masculinities." In *Progressive Black Masculinities,* edited by Athena D. Mutua. New York: Routledge, 2006.

———. *Black Sexual Politics.* New York: Routledge, 2004.

Hughes, Langston. "The Negro Artist and the Racial Mountain." In Angelyn Mitchell, ed., *Within the Circle.*

Hurston, Zora Neal. *Dust Tracks on a Road: An Autobiography.* New York: HarperCollins, 1996.

———. *Their Eyes Were Watching God.* New York: Perennial Library, 1990.

Ikard, David. *Breaking the Silence: Toward a Black Male Feminist Criticism.* Baton Rouge: Louisiana State University Press, 2007.

———. "Ruthless Individuality and the Other(ed) Black Women in Zora Neale Hurston's *Their Eyes Were Watching God.*" CLA *Journal* 53 (2009): 1–22.

Ikard, David H., and Martel Lee Teasley. *Nation of Cowards: Black Activism in Barack Obama's Post-Racial America.* Bloomington: Indiana University Press, 2012.

Jami. January 16, 2010 (4:13 PM), comment on R. Kamille Williams, "A Black Princess," *Office of Black Church Studies at Duke University Divinity School Blog,* January 10, 2010.

Johnson, James Weldon. *Autobiography of an Ex-Colored Man.* Charleston: Biblio-Bazaar, 2009.

Jones, Edward P. *The Known World.* New York: Harper Collins, 2003.

———. "We Tell Stories." Original Essays, Powell's Books website. Accessed July 21, 2009, http://www.powells.com/fromtheauthor/jones.html.

———. Interview by Maryemma Graham. *African American Review* 42.3–4 (Fall/Winter 2008): 421–438.

Lorde, Audre, "The Master's Tools Will Never Dismantle the Master's House." In *Sister Outsider: Essays and Speeches.* Berkeley: The Crossing Press, 1984.

———. "The Transformation of Silence Into Language and Action." In *Sister Outsider: Essays and Speeches.* Berkeley: Crossing Press, 1984.

Marshall, Paule. *Praisesong for a Widow.* New York: Plume, 1984.

McBride, Dwight. *Why I Hate Abercrombie and Fitch: Essays on Race and Sexuality.* New York: New York University Press, 2005.

Mercer, Kobena. *Welcome to the Jungle: New Positions in Black Cultural Studies.* London: Routledge, 1994.

Mirkinson, Jack. "CNN Suspends Roland Martin For 'Offensive' Super BowlTweets." *Huffington Post,* first posted Feb. 12, 2012; updated Feb. 9, 2012, http://www.huffingtonpost.com/2012/02/08/roland-martin-suspended-cnn-super-bowl_n_1263276.html.

Mitchell, Angelyn. *Within the Circle: An Anthology of African American Literary Criticism from the Harlem Renaissance to the Present.* Durham: Duke University Press, 1994.

Morgan, Joan. *When Chickenheads Come Home to Roost: A Hip Hop Feminist Breaks It Down.* New York: Touchstone, 2000.

Morrison, Toni. *Beloved.* New York: Penguin Books, 1987.

———. *Playing in the Dark: Whiteness and the Literary Imagination.* New York: Vintage, 1992.

———. *The Bluest Eye.* New York: Alfred A. Knopf, 2000.

———. "Unspeakable Things Unspoken: The Afro-American Presence in African American Literature." In Angelyn Mitchell, ed., *Within the Circle.*

Murray, Rolland. "Black Crisis Shuffle: Fiction, Race, and Simulation." *African American Review* 42.2 (Summer 2008): 215–233.

Mutua, Athena D. *Progressive Black Masculinities.* New York: Routledge, 2006.

Neal, Mark Anthony. *New Black Man.* New York: Routledge Press, 2005.

Nelly, "Tip Drill." *Before Da Kappa 2K4.* Swishahouse, 2008. Compact disc.

Newitz, Annalee, and Matthew Wray. "What is 'White Trash'?: Stereotypes and Economic Conditions of Poor Whites in the United States." In *Whiteness: A Critical Reader,* edited by Mike Hill. New York: New York University Press, 1997. 168–186.

Norton, Michael L., and Samuel R. Sommers. "Whites See Racism as a Zero-Sum Game That They Are Now Losing." *Perspectives on Psychological Science* 215 (2011): 215–218.

Obama, Barack. *The Audacity of Hope: Thoughts on Reclaiming the American Dream.* New York: Random House, 2006.

Obama, Michelle. Interview by Steve Kroft. *60 Minutes.* CBS. February 11, 2007.

Pitts, Martha. "Happy-To-Be-Nappy Barbie," *Ms. Magazine Blog,* December 22, 2011, http://msmagazine.com/blog/blog/2011/12/22/happy-to-be-nappy-barbie.

Powers, Nicholas. "'Precious' or How I Learned to Stop Worrying and Love the Movie." *The Indypendent,* December 8, 2009, http://www.indypendent.org/2009/12/08/precious-or-how-i-learned-stop-worrying-and-love-movie.

Pyun, Jeanie. Review of *The White Boy Shuffle,* by Paul Beatty. *Salon.com,* June 6, 1996, http://www.salon.com/writer/jeanie_pyun.html.

Reed, Ishmael. "Fade to White." *New York Times,* February 4, 2010, http://www.nytimes.com/2010/02/05/opinion/05reed.html.

———. "The Selling of Precious." *Counter Punch,* December 4, 2009, http://www.counterpunch.org/2009/12/04/the-selling-of-quot-precious-quot/.

Rock, Chris. *Bigger and Blacker*. Directed by Keith Truesdell. New York: HBO Home Video, 1999. DVD.

Roediger, David R. *How Race Survived U.S. History: From Settlement and Slavery to the Obama Phenomenon*. New York: Verso, 2010.

"Santaluces High School in Florida on Alert after 2 Teens Post Racist Video," *Huffington Post*, Feb. 21, 2012.

Sapphire. PUSH. New York: Random House, 1996.

Schuyler, George. *Black No More*. New York: Dover, 2011.

Sharpley-Whiting, Tracey Denean. *Pimps Up, Ho's Down: Hip Hop's Hold on Young Black Women*. New York: New York University Press, 2007.

Soulja Boy. *The DeAndre Way*. Interscope Records, 2010. Compact disc.

Stallings, L. H. "Punked For Life: Paul Beatty's *The White Boy Shuffle* and Radical Black Masculinities." *African American Review* 43.1 (Spring 2009): 99–116.

Szalavitz, Maia. "Study: Whites More Likely to Abuse Drugs Than Blacks." *Time.com*, November 7, 2011, http://healthland.time.com/2011/11/07/study-whites-more-likely-to-abuse-drugs-than-blacks/.

United States Department of Labor, Office of Policy Planning and Research. March, 1965. *The Negro Family: The Case for National Action*, http://www.dol.gov/oasam/programs/history/webid-meynihan.htm [This address is correct despite the spelling "meynihan"].

Washington, Harriet A. *Medical Apartheid: The Dark History of Medical Experimentation on Black Americans from Colonial Times to the Present*. New York: Anchor, 2006.

White, Armond. "Pride and Precious." Review of the movie *Precious*, directed by Lee Daniels. *New York Press*, November 4, 2009, http://www.nypress.com/article-20554-pride-precious.html.

Wise, Tim. *Between Barack and a Hard Place: Racism and White Denial in the Age of Obama*. San Francisco: City Lights, 2009.

Wolfe, George C. *The Colored Museum*. New York: Grove Press, 1994.

Wright, Richard. "Between Laughter and Tears." *New Masses*, October 5, 1937, 22–23.

Yeager, Patricia. *Dirt and Desire: Reconstructing Southern Women's Writing, 1930–1990*. Chicago: University of Chicago Press, 2000.

Index

accommodationism: black, 151–152; blind, 155

acting white, 99

activism, 14, 19; community, 69; scholar-, 18

African: "black as an," 145; captives, 114; colonialism, 70; diaspora, 112; features, 73, 116–117; Ibos, 147; indentured servants, 158n5; lighter skinned, 115; women, 115. *See also* African Americans; beauty; skin/skinned; slavery

African Americans: and black authenticity, 72, 152; and black feminism, 13, 47, 50–55, 59, 89, 93, 100, 141; and black nationalism, 72; and black realities, 135; and colloquialism, 101; class elitism, 134, 137, 139; concept of blackness, 145; and culture, 145; and culpability, 16, 25, 115, 133; debate over *Precious,* 143–149 (*see also* Precious); faith in white goodwill, as dangerous, 152; and history, 133, 145; and ideals of beauty, 105–106; and hair, 110, 112, 113–114; and literature, 100, 133; male leaders, 122; male privilege, 159n6; and popular culture, 116, 125; queer, 13, 82, 87–89, 92, 93, 94, 95, 96, 141, 159n6, 162n16; and representation in movies, 127–128; and Santa Claus, 146; and satire, 68; as slave-owners, 16, 24; taboos, 89, 94; women, 116; and violence, 72, 109. *See also* beauty; elites; pop culture; rape; womanhood

African Americans, as pathological, 2, 4, 10, 14, 43, 68, 75, 88, 110, 118, 132; angry and violent, 89; and behavior, 25, 74–76; discourse, 12, 16; and mindset, 23; and notions, 18; and self-hate, 27; whites' obsession with stereotypes of, 134. *See also* pathology

anti-white bias, 107

Autobiography of an Ex-Colored Man (Johnson), 137

Awkward, Michael, 51

Baldwin, James, 25, 59, 102, 107, 112, 127

Bamboozled (Lee), 134, 158n13

Barbies, 126–127, 129

Bassard, Katherine Clay, 22

Beatty, Paul, 9–10, 16–17, 65, 67–68

beauty, 17, 105, 108–113, 116, 120, 124–126, 129; and black, 105, 114; and ideal, 108; and white, 115, 19, 121–123, 125; and white standards of, 111; and white women's, 128

Beloved (Morrison), 11, 16, 42, 45, 47, 50, 62

Birth of a Nation (Griffith), 97, 140

blacks. *See* African Americans

"Black Crisis Shuffle: Fiction, Race, and Simulation," (Murray), 81

Black No More (Schuyler), 122

Blind Side, The (John Lee Hancock), 132

blindness, 57, 108, 152; gendered, 50; patriarchal, 57; white, 134; willful, 2, 37

Blow, Charles M., 90–91, 141–142, 144

Bluest Eye, The (Morrison), 104, 123–124

Boondocks (McGrudger), 158n13

Bonilla-Silva, Eduardo, 108

Boyz n the Hood, 60